SACRED FIRE

By Ron and Ryan Sutton

Unless otherwise indicated, all Scripture quotations are taken from the King James Version (KJV) of the Bible.

SACRED FIRE

ISBN: 978-1483980928

Copyright © 2013 by Ron and Ryan Sutton

ABOUT THE AUTHORS

Ron Sutton was converted from a life of crime and drug abuse during the Jesus Movement in 1972. His ministry has taken him to sixty nations. He has conducted mass crusades and leaders' conferences, served as a missionary, evangelist, pastor and church planter. His books on evangelism, gospel tracts and pro-life literature have been distributed throughout the USA and internationally. He and his wife Cindy established a drug rehabilitation ministry, a childrens' home in Costa Rica, and a home for unwed mothers. Ron served as director of the School of Christ International in Africa. He is currently planting a church near St. Louis, while continuing to travel in ministry, and assist his son Ryan at The Grace Center.

Ryan Sutton surrendered to the call to preach under the ministry of B.H. Clendennen a few days after his fourteenth birthday in 1997. He preached his first sermon the following Sunday and was ordained to pastor his first church three years later. He has preached in churches and revivals throughout the USA and has ministered internationally in China, Russia, India, Europe, Africa and Latin America. Ryan continues to travel and preach throughout the nation while serving as the senior pastor of The Grace Center, a dynamic multi-cultural church, in Festus, Missouri.

TO ORDER MATERIALS OR SCHEDULE MEETINGS
The Grace Center
P.O. Box 21, Crystal City, Missouri 63019
636-465-0885
www.TheGraceCenter.com | www.RyanSutton.org

CONTENTS

FOREWORD

"Why don't we try Pentecost one more time?"

(B.H. Clendennen)

The greatest need of the modern church is a fresh baptism of the Holy Ghost and fire – a whole-hearted return to the power and passion of Pentecost. The pulpits of America are filled with preachers who have never been baptized with the Holy Spirit. They think a degree from a university or a piece of paper from an organization qualifies them to preach. That idea didn't come from the Bible. Jesus didn't tell the apostles to wait in Jerusalem until they could put letters behind their names. (We esteem education. We have degrees, but that does not qualify us to preach). Jesus didn't say "wait until headquarters gives you a license to do what I have commanded." Jesus said to wait for the promise of the Father – the Baptism of the Holy Spirit:

"And, being assembled together with them, commanded them that they should not depart from Jerusalem, but wait for the promise of the Father, which saith he, ye have heard of me. For John truly baptized with water, but ye shall be baptized with the Holy Ghost not many days hence" (Acts 1: 4, 5).

We should note that Jesus himself did not begin his public ministry until the Spirit came on him: *"Now when all the people were baptized, it came to pass, that Jesus also being baptized, and praying, the heaven was opened, and the Holy Ghost descended in a bodily shape like a dove upon him, and a voice came from heaven, which said, Thou art my beloved son; in thee I am well pleased... And Jesus being full of the Holy Ghost returned from Jordan, and was led by the Spirit into the wilderness... And Jesus returned in the power of the Spirit into Galilee: and there went out a fame of him through all the region round about. And he came to Nazareth where he had been brought up: and, as his custom was, he went into the synagogue on the Sabbath day, and stood up for to read. And there was delivered unto him the book of the prophet Esaias. And when he had opened the book, he found the place where it was written, The Spirit of the LORD is upon me, because he hath anointed me to preach the Gospel to the poor, He hath sent me to heal the brokenhearted, to preach deliverance to the captives, and recovering of sight to the blind, to set at liberty them that are bruised, to preach the acceptable year of the Lord"* (Luke 3:21-22; 4:1, 14-19).

It is clear that Jesus expected his disciples to follow the same pattern: A heavenly call followed by a baptism of power was required before entering public ministry. *"But ye shall receive power, after that the Holy Ghost has come upon you: and ye shall be witnesses unto me... And when the day of Pentecost was fully come, they were all with one accord in one place. And suddenly there came a sound from heaven as of a rushing mighty wind, and it filled all the house where they were sitting. And there appeared unto them cloven tongues like as of fire, and it sat on upon each of them. And they were all filled with the Holy Ghost, and began to speak with other tongues, as the Spirit gave them utterance"* (Acts 1:8; 2:1-4).

Those spirit-baptized preachers went out of the Upper Room preaching a gospel of power with tongues of fire. The greatest period of growth in the history of the church followed. Few preachers in our day imitate that pattern. We had the privilege of working with one who did, B.H. Clendennen, a true soldier of the Cross who highly esteemed the power of Pentecost. I was honored to serve under his leadership as director of the School of Christ in Africa. He spent his eightieth birthday with us in Lusaka, Zambia. For six days, he taught some six hundred leaders morning and night – up to eight hours a day. I don't think it was humanly possible for an eighty year old preacher to begin each day praying at 5:30 a.m. and then teach – actually, preach hard for up to eight hours. He did it by the "life of Another." He did it through the power of the Holy Ghost.

We recall that he ended many of his teachings at that conference (as he did all over the world) with the words:

"Why don't we try Pentecost one more time?"

He practiced what he preached. He tried Pentecost throughout nearly sixty years of ministry. He was converted after fighting as a Marine in World War II and filled with the Holy Ghost soon thereafter. He launched the School of Christ and went as a missionary to Russia at the age of seventy-one. The organization with which he was affiliated told him they would not send him: he was too old. He went anyway and, because of the power of Pentecost operating through his life, the School of Christ was established in over one-hundred-twenty nations. He greatly impacted our lives – and the lives of thousands of preachers around the world. He preached with force well into his eighties because he never deviated from the message or power of Pentecost.

In the 1970's, a well-known Charismatic leader was called "Mr. Pentecost." We think the men who truly deserve that title are David Wilkerson and B.H. Clendennen. They had deep respect for one another. I spent some time with Wilkerson at a leaders' conference in Africa. When he learned that I worked with Clendennen he smiled, looked heavenward for a moment and said, "He's one of the old soldiers. There aren't many of us left."

The impact of B.H. Clendennen on our lives re-shaped our values, strengthened our convictions, and literally altered the course of our ministries. We pray that, at least in some small way, the power of a man who "lived by the life of Another" will be released in the pages of this book. If the message of this book bears witness to your spirit, we ask you to join us in our quest to recover the passion and power of the early church.

"Why don't we try Pentecost one more time?"

Chapter One

Sacred Fire

The Baptism of the Holy Ghost is more than a baptism of power. It is a baptism of life, of love, of fire. In the holy fire of the Spirit's presence, pure life and passionate love are released. Fruit is the expression of life. Love is the fruit of the Spirit. This life, the Pentecostal life, is fueled by fire from heaven. Purity, power, and passion – all are released as the holy fire of heaven burns in our hearts. The love that comes with the life is released as the holy fire of heaven burns in our hearts. The love that comes with the life is filled with passion and fervent desire. It leads us to the altar of supreme devotion where we "*present our bodies a living sacrifice*" (Romans 12:1). On this holy altar of surrender and service, we exchange our lowly life for His glorious life.

Upon rising from this flaming altar, we are consumed by the passion of holy love burning in our hearts. We are no longer our own. We have laid down our life and now, "*it is Christ that liveth in me*" (Galatians 2:20). We are willing to spend and be spent in joyful service to our King. The cry of our heart has become, "make me thy fuel, thou Flame of God."

Fire! Holy fire, burning in the hearts of people alive with passion for God, is the essence of authentic Christianity. Holy fire from heaven burning in our hearts purifies the whole being and opens the way for a greater outpouring of power, life, and love. Rising from the flaming altar of consecration and surrender, we encounter the Holy Ghost in greater measure- in deeper dimension.

"...the love of God is shed abroad in our hearts by the Holy Ghost which is given unto us" (Romans 5:5).

There is no excitement in half-hearted commitment. There is no passion in the relationship where the heart is not given fully to another. Passion thrives on the fuel of unselfish love which is given without reservation to the one I love. The fire of love burns most brightly when I give full release to my emotions, when my heart is no longer my own, when I hold nothing back. The fire of holy passion burns most fervently in the heart that is consumed with love.

This is the problem with much of modern Christianity. Our hearts are not burning with the fire of holy love because we hold ourselves back from the One who loves us. We fear to give our hearts completely to Him. The love of the world and the things of the world claim part of our heart. Holy fire will never fall on a divided heart.

"And thou shalt love the Lord thy God with all thy heart, and with all thy soul, and with al thy mind, and with all they strength" (Mark 12:30).

If we love God in this way, with all our being, we will pour our hearts out in love until there is nothing left to give. We will hold nothing back. We will gladly empty ourselves. We will joyfully break the alabaster box and pour out all the treasure we once held dear in extravagant, unselfish worship. It is here at the place of emptiness, that we will encounter fullness. It is when the vessel is empty that the oil of heaven is poured out. It is here at this holy place of extravagant worship that the love of God is shed abroad in our hearts. It is here that we experience an overwhelming fullness that moves the heart to sing, *"It is joy unspeakable and full of glory"* (I Peter 1:8).

It is when we empty ourselves, when we come as empty vessels desiring to be filled with nothing but Him, that we discover, *"In His presence is fullness of joy and at His right hand are pleasure forevermore"* (Psalms 16:11). It is at this place, where the fullness of heaven surges through our being searching out every empty place, that we taste the true sweetness of the heavenly gifts. It is here, with the holy fire burning in our hearts, that we *"Set our affections on things above, not on things on the earth"* (Colossians 3:2). The power of the world is broken. Holy love has conquered worldly lust. Holy fire has sanctified and set us apart. Another world has claimed us. *"Ye are dead, and your life is hid with Christ in God"* (Colossians 3:3).

I have exchanged my lowly life for His glorious life. I am now *"crucified with Christ; nevertheless I live; yet not I, but Christ liveth in me..."* (Galatians 2:20). I now live by the life of another. I have become a vessel, a holy vessel that Christ flows through. It is on this holy life from heaven that fire can fall. It is to this life that power can be entrusted. It is through this life that love in all its fullness can flow.

The wind and fire that brought a baptism of power and love to the Upper Room found one-hundred-twenty empty vessels. To the natural eye, the Upper Room was a pitiful site. There was no life there. The occupants were discouraged, confused, and fearful. Their hopes were crushed by the Crucifixion of Christ. Their dreams had died with Him. Filled with despair, their hearts feared to believe the reports of the Resurrection (Mark 16:15).

How suddenly the atmosphere changed! Emptiness was just what the Spirit needed. Heaven's fullness always comes to empty vessels who are left with nothing but desire for God.

"And suddenly there came a sound from heaven, as of a rushing mighty wind, and it filled the whole house where they were sitting. Then there appeared to them cloven tongues, as of fire, and one sat upon each of them. And they were all filled with the Holy Spirit and began to speak with other tongues, as the Spirit gave them utterance" (Acts 2:2-4).

And suddenly, the wind blew, the fire fell, the power was poured out! And suddenly, fearful disciples were transformed into courageous preachers. And suddenly, heaven invaded earth and the Holy Spirit took up residence in the hearts of men.

God answered the cry of emptiness with holy fire. *"He shall baptize you with the Holy Ghost and with fire"* (Matthew 3:11). Holy fire is the chosen symbol of His presence. John saw

Jesus walking among the seven golden candlesticks which represented the churches. Jesus warned the church in Ephesus to repent *"or else I will come and remove they candlestick"* (Revelation 1:20 and 2:5). When the fire is removed, the Presence departs. How we need to repent and return to our first love. How careful we must be to fan the flames and be ever watchful to keep our first love burning with passion and zeal.

Nothing of earth can help us. Our crying need is for Holy Ghost fire coming down from heaven. We are in danger. How long will we tolerate this sterile romance with lukewarm Christianity? How long will we refuse God all our heart? If we will empty ourselves, if we will set our affections on things above, the fire will fall. Our stale religion will be replaced with abundant life; our weakness will be exchanged for power from on high, and the joy of His presence will fill our hearts. Why do we wait? Why do we hold ourselves back from the one who loves us? Why don't we try Pentecost one more time?

Chapter Two

Science and the Supernatural

There is no dichotomy between science and the supernatural. True science is not the enemy of faith: it supports it. There is no conflict between Bible truth and scientific fact. But in the western world we carefully separate the two, largely because our minds are more conditioned by myths like evolution than by real science. We are suspicious of the supernatural because our secular minds have been shaped by *"oppositions of science falsely so called"* (1 Timothy 6:20). We look for something tangible that can be felt, smelled, seen, tasted, or heard. We place great confidence in our natural senses but fail to develop the spiritual sense of faith. We revolt against the Bible revelation that the natural world emerged from the spiritual, that visible things were created from invisible.

The Bible is emphatic about its statements of truth concerning creation. There is no argument between real science and Bible truth, between revelation received by faith and discovery obtained by true science. *"In the beginning was the Word, and the Word was with God, and the Word was God...All* things were made by him..." (John 1:1,3). *"Through faith we understand that the worlds were framed by the word of God, so that things which are seen were not made of things that do appear* (Hebrews 11:3).

Dogmatic teachers of religion insist that the heavens and the earth were created in six literal twenty-four hour days. The secular, scientific mind flatly rejects the idea.

The spiritually perceptive are not so dogmatic because they remember that *"with the Lord a day is as a thousand years and a thousand years as a day"* (2 Peter 3:8). Many of the conflicts between science and the supernatural result from narrowness of thought. In time, all conflicts will be resolved because science and truth both originate from the same source; both point to one Creator. The reality is that we need both faith and spiritual enlightenment to properly understand the scientific, and to correctly perceive the supernatural. We need the help of the Holy Spirit who will saturate us with the light of truth: *"Howbeit when he, the Spirit of truth is come, he will guide you into all truth: for he shall not speak of himself; but whatsoever he shall hear, that shall he speak: and he will show you things to come"* (John 16:13).

We desperately need the power of the Holy Spirit in the western church, but our so-called secular, scientific minds are reticent to receive it. Those who understand the need for renewed emphasis on the power of the Holy Spirit must pray for the modern church which is often void of real spiritual power. We must pray for enlightenment, for without enlightenment the church will never perceive her need for the power of the Spirit. *"...making mention of you in my prayers; the eyes of your understanding being enlightened; that you may know...what is the exceeding greatness of his power to us-ward who believe, according to the working of his mighty power"* (Ephesians 1:16-19). Enlightenment will cause us to once again cry out for a fresh baptism with the Holy Spirit. Faith will find power to deliver the church from her impotence. Faith will send her into the world with the same anointing that was on Jesus: *"How God anointed Jesus of Nazareth with the Holy Ghost and with power: who went about doing good, and healing all that were oppressed of the devil; for God was with him"* (Acts 10:38).

Jesus told His disciples that all power in heaven and earth had been given unto Him, and then He told them to go with that power and preach the gospel (Matthew 28:18-19).

They waited for that power as He instructed (Luke 24:49) and they went out to preach as He commanded: "…*and they went forth, and preached everywhere, the Lord working with them, and confirming the word with signs following*" (Mark 16:20).

We would see those same signs if we would go out filled with the same power. We need a fresh anointing. Why don't we try Pentecost one more time?

The university professor was a deacon at a large Baptist church. Why he was showing the most convincing video on evolution ever produced, I could not imagine. I was shocked at the conclusion of the presentation to hear him say, "I will not permit discussion on opposing views. I just wanted you to see that there is scientific support for the theory of evolution."

Scientific support for an unproved theory? Scientific support for a theory not believed by the bored mind that spawned it? Scientific support for speculation and imagination? I admitted that the video was highly professional and excellently produced, but I saw no real science in it. That's why I raised my hand and said "Excuse me, professor."

Most of the students were young people concerned about their grades and intimidated by their professors. I was forty-two and, for some reason, back at the university knocking out another degree. To meet the requirements for that degree, I found myself in a class on anthropology watching a film on evolution. I was not concerned about my grades (I graduated summa cum laude). I was not intimidated by the professor. "Excuse me, professor, but I do not intend to be censored. I do have an opposing view and I wish to discuss it." He responded, "There will be no discussion. This is my class, I establish the rules here." I replied, "I, along with many other property owners in this county, pay your salary. I am also a Christian minister with strong convictions about freedom of speech."

I didn't want to be difficult, nor did I want to be silenced. After a bit of bantering back and forth, the professor surmised that his attempts at intimidation had failed and he reluctantly said, "All right. Let's hear your response." Without hesitation I commented, "I find no scientific support for evolution. The theory rests on speculation and assumption." I concluded by stating, "It would take a great deal more faith for me to believe the myth of evolution that to believe the fact of creation."

After the class, several Christian students thanked me for taking a stand and two apologized for not speaking up. Why are Christians afraid of science, afraid to challenge a faulty theory falsely called science? Real science has no argument with the Bible. They support one another.

At the conclusion of a lecture to several hundred teen-age boys at a Russian technical school in 1991, I was asked this question: "Do you believe the world came into being through the process of evolution?" I responded by pointing to a painting and asking, "Do you believe that for this painting to exist an artist had to at one time exist?" Following an enthusiastic, affirmative response, I went on, "When I look at the beauty and order of Creation, I know that a Creator must exist. If you don't believe that a painting can be created by chance, how can you believe that the universe came into being without the planning and intelligent design of a Creator?

This is not a book on Creation, but on the Spirit of Creation. It is about the power of Pentecost, about the supernatural power of the Spirit operating in the lives of believers. The supernatural has no argument with science. However, the scientific western mind has a lot of problems with the supernatural. Only spiritual enlightenment will erase the question marks imprinted on our minds by unproved theories. To begin our study on the power of Pentecost, we will locate the Spirit of Pentecost at the beginning of the Bible. We find Him moving with creative power in complete harmony with real science.

"In the beginning God created the heaven and the earth. And the earth was without form, and void, and darkness was upon the face of the deep. And the Spirit of God moved upon the face of the waters" (Genesis 1:1-2).

The same Spirit who moved upon the face of the waters in Genesis became living water in John 7:38-39: *"He that believeth on me, as the scripture hath said, out of his belly shall flow rivers of living water. But this spake he of the Spirit, which they that believe on him should receive:"* The same Spirit who brought order out of chaos at the birth of the earth brought power at the birth of the church.

"And when the day of Pentecost was fully come they were all with

one accord in one place. And suddenly there came a sound from heaven as of a rushing mighty wind, and it filled all the house where they were sitting. And there appeared unto them cloven tongues like as of fire, and it sat upon each of them. And they were all filled with the Holy Ghost and began to speak with other tongues, as the Spirit gave them utterance" (Acts 2:1-4).

The Holy Spirit was present in power at the birth of the world and the birth of the church, at Creation and at Pentecost. This book is written to the end that we might restore the message and recover the power of Pentecost. The church is a chaotic mass of disjointed members without the Spirit brooding over us. We are helpless without Him. The church was born in Pentecostal power. The church Jesus returns for will be filled with that same power. There is no contradiction between science and the supernatural.

We in the western world must not allow our suspicion of the supernatural to hinder our pursuit of the Holy Spirit. We desperately need power. Why don't we try Pentecost one more time?

Chapter Three

The Gospel of Life

Can our gospel stand up under the scientific search for fact? Not if it comes out of a religious system which is dogmatically imposed on life. It can, if instead of coming from a system which stands outside of life, it comes up out of life. The gospel has no conflict with scientific fact. True science supports and confirms it. There is no need for the glorious life, out of which the gospel flows, to concern itself with theories and suppositions of science. It lays hold of eternal facts and realities. It has no time to entertain an empty theory like evolution for it has, by faith, already taken hold of the divine fact of creation.

This life is not confused by even the highest human intellectual reasonings. It is not intimidated by oppositions of "science falsely so-called." It holds its ground before all the shallow arguments of men for it is governed by the mind of Christ. It answers every question, silences every argument, because this life is a Person, and this Person is Truth. All the clouds of confusion are dispelled when we give ourselves to this life and arrive at the understanding that *"In Him we live and more and have our being"* (Acts 17:8).

The gospel is founded in fact—the fact of Christ. This fact stands behind science. It has no conflict with it. And if followed to their correct conclusion, scientific facts will always lead us to the central fact of our moral and spiritual universe—Christ. His gospel is not a theory borrowed from the brain of an earth-bound scientist; nor is it a collection of ideas issuing from the thoughts of a lifeless philosopher; it came out of life and, armed with the facts of life, it always leads to life.

How we have harmed the gospel. When people encountered Christ in the flesh, they were confronted by life and power. What do they encounter for the most part today? The gospel has been buried beneath religious routine and ritual. The life has been suppressed by priests and preachers who are lifeless because they have never surrendered to the source of life. Christianity is not a religion. It is a life lived in the power of the Spirit. We do not need a new movement of religion. We need a new discovery of Christ, a fresh revelation of life. We need to uncover and re-introduce to this world the true gospel of life.

Only Christ, the Giver of life, can answer the questions

of the mortal mind and satisfy the longings of the hu

heart. The One who said, *"I am the way, the truth, and th*

(John 14:6) has not left us alone to stumble through the

darkness of this world. He has sent an emissary from another

world, the precious Holy Spirit, the spirit of life, who makes

the Bible live. Led by the spirit, we come to the Bible, not just

for knowledge but for life.

"According as his divine power has given us all things that pertain unto life and godliness, through the knowledge of him that has called us to glory and virtue. Whereby are given unto us exceeding great and precious promises that by these ye might be partakers of the divine nature, having escaped the corruption that is in the world through lust" (2 Peter 1:3-4).

The central issue is life. Knowledge which does not lead to life is empty and useless. At the end of the journey, it is life, not knowledge, which will lift us out of the corruption of this world.

Meaning and purpose can never be found in the cold world of scientific fact. They must be discovered in the warm world of spiritual life. It is futile to search for answers apart from life. They are not found in the realm of human thought but in the higher realm of divine revelation. Ultimate truth is not found in the world of science. It is revealed in the world of the Spirit. Science which stands in contradiction of spiritual truth is not true science. All that is truly factual leads to the central fact of our moral and spiritual universe—a Person who is truth. Christ, who is the way, the truth, and the life, has sent forth the Holy Spirit who will lead us into all truth (John 16:13).

Truth is revealed, and life is manifest, in those who receive the spirit of truth. Truth is imparted, and life is produced, in those whose searching leads them to a Person. Truth is the revelation of the person of Christ. Life is relationship with Him.

The gospel meets the demand of inquisitive minds for scientific fact. It also answers the cry of the human heart for meaningful experience. The Christianity modeled by Christ is charged with life, power, and energy. The life in the gospel will not sit down quietly and reverently in the whitewashed sepulchers of religion. It refuses to comfortably settle into worn-out ritual, narrow dogmatism, and empty tradition. It demands an atmosphere of energy where truth can be expressed, where power can be released and God can be experienced.

Youth in our Bible schools and universities are becoming old before their time for lack of vital experience. They are bored by study which produces knowledge that is not put into practice. In the sterile environment of higher learning they are ever learning but never coming to the knowledge of the truth. Why? Because they sit under the influence of professors who deny the power of the gospel. They long for study which leads not to religious theory, but to practical experience. The hunger is not to know more about God. The cry is *"that I might know Him"* in vital experience. The hungry have no more appetite for religious debate and endless theories. They want to live. They want to experience the power of life.

The true gospel has experience at its heart. Jesus didn't lead with theories. His teaching pointed to and merged with experience. His followers didn't call people to theories but to life. They didn't proclaim "that which we have studied and learned declare we unto you". Listen to John's cry: *"that which we have seen and heard declare we unto you."* The gospel Christ preached is charged with the energy of spiritual experience: *"The words that I speak to you, they are spirit, and they are life"* (John 6:63). His gospel advocated experiencing life in the fullest measure: *"I am come that you might have life and have it more abundantly"* (John 10:10).

The teaching of Jesus produced experience, not theory. His followers didn't know about God. They knew Him. They didn't imagine what resurrection might be like. They knew. The Resurrection was with them. They weren't waiting to experience eternal life. It had already entered into them. All their study and learning led to experience. It was practically expressed in life. Study was exciting because they knew that around the next bend in the road what they had recently learned would be transformed into experience. There was excitement and energy because they were "learning of Him," and all their learning led to life and experience.

The modern world is weary of both secular materialism and religious dogmatism. This generation is looking for something that is alive, something that will inject meaning into its empty existence. The church must recover a testimony of power if it is to impact this age: a testimony of power that flows out of life. A generation that demands experience will never be moved by the letter of the law. There must be a manifestation of the Spirit. The demand for experience leads straight to Pentecost. The church which answers the demands of science and experience is the church of the Upper Room, a Pentecostal church which preaches a gospel of life and power, a gospel which is demonstrated in the real world of human experience. Why don't we try Pentecost one more time?

"And my speech and my preaching was not with enticing words of man's wisdom, but in demonstration of the Spirit and of power: That your faith should not stand in the wisdom of men, but in the power of God" (1 Corinthians 2:4-5).

Chapter Four

Why Don't We Try Pentecost One More Time?

The Western Church is compromised. A return to
Pentecost is imperative. Without the sacred fire and
supernatural power of Pentecost, history will repeat and the
modern church will be engulfed in darkness – a horrible,
aggressive darkness reminiscent of the Dark Ages.

The end of the age is upon us. Jesus warned that in the
last days evil would increase. The coming flood of evil must
be met with power. The dark hordes of hell will laugh at a
worldly church. Half-hearted Christians will be devoured by a
whole-hearted devil.

The modern church has embraced a watered-down,
materialistic gospel. Preachers have cared more for popularity
and prosperity than for real power. The pulpit is largely to
blame for the debility of the church. New Testament
preachers had tongues of fire. Modern preachers have
tongues of silk. These smooth-talking, popularity seekers are
always willing to scratch itching ears. They can't raise their

voices in thunderous proclamation of a holy gospel because they have no fire.

Where there is no fire there is no power nor authority to deal with the darkness. I do not want to hear a demon say to me what the seven sons of Sceva heard: "*Jesus we know and Paul we know, but who are you*" (Acts 19:14). Paul was known in hell because he embraced, preached and lived the real gospel. When he spoke to demons they listened. They knew him because he knew who he was – who he was in Jesus. His gospel was not with "*enticing words of man's wisdom, but in demonstration of the spirit and of power*" (I Corinthians 2:4).

The devil backs up for nothing but the power of the Spirit and the authority of Jesus. A man's authority is in the word he speaks. "*...but speak the word only and my servant shall be healed*" (Matthew 8:8). The power of God is available today, as it was to the believers in the Book of Acts – but it is not available to those who are willing to compromise and preach a watered-down-gospel. If we are thinking clearly, we will not trade power for popularity.

Why do we play the game of religion while the door of Pentecost remains open to us? Why are we hesitant to take our hands off and fully yield to the Holy Spirit once again? Have we lost our ability to trust Him? The Apostle Paul was careful about touching Holy things. He wanted to bring order to the Corinthian church – but not at the expense of a loss of freedom and power. The easy road is to take control ourselves, create a comfortable atmosphere and design services that will appeal to and entertain the "seekers." The easy road is not the best road.

I want no part of a philosophy of ministry which allows a human being to dictate when and how the precious Holy Spirit may move in a meeting. I want Him to return in fullness. I love Him. I need Him. God forbid that I should place any limits on Him. I want the passion and love of the Holy Spirit to burn in me. I want to be a man with a tongue of fire. I humbly pray, "Make me thy fuel, thou flame of God."

Permit me to ask this question: Why would we want to trade the power and excitement of Pentecost for the sterile environment of modern, "seeker friendly" religion?

Why? Have we become too concerned about our own comfort and security? Is it possible that in our carnality we have come to the point of being ashamed of the real gospel – the gospel proclaimed in power with glorious manifestations of the Holy Spirit? I humbly suggest that we return to Pentecost and boldly proclaim with the Apostle Paul,

"For I am not ashamed of the gospel of Christ: for it is the power of God unto salvation to everyone that believeth..." (Romans 1:16).

In this book, we want to do more than suggest that we return to Pentecost. We want to plead with every believer who has grieved the Holy Spirit by restricting His movement, to return to the fullness we once knew. We have grieved Him by failing to trust Him – by failing to yield to Him. Pastors throughout America have stood in their pulpits and made announcements similar to this: "Verbal manifestations of the Holy Spirit will no longer be allowed in our Sunday worship services." Once vibrant churches where gifts of the Spirit operated and hungry believers filled altars to seek the baptism of the Spirit, now conduct entertaining – but powerless-- meetings. Was it worth the trade?

Silk-tongued, smooth-talking motivational speakers are ill equipped to prepare God's people for the coming storm. The only hope for the Church is true, heaven-sent revival. That revival must begin in the pulpit with men who find a tongue of fire: fire which enables them to once again preach with passion and power. We need to try Pentecost one more time.

A watered-down gospel has little power to convict of sin. Where there is no conviction, there is no repentance. Where there is no repentance, there is no conversion. Where there is no conversion, there are no real Christians. What happens when a person who has never heard the real gospel, has never been convicted, has never repented of sin, prays to receive Jesus? Is it not ministerial malpractice to lead someone in a "sinner's prayer" who has never been convinced that he is a sinner in need of a Savior? Yet this takes place in churches and on radio and television throughout America every week. Are we filling church buildings with believers or tares?

How unlike John the Baptist and Jesus we have become; how unlike the apostles and preaching deacons of the early church. They knew nothing about creating a comfortable atmosphere for sinful seekers. They went out of their churches looking for sinners to confront them and to challenge them to repent. If anything, they made them uncomfortable. But the results were glorious! Convicted sinners repented and became converted Christians. Manifestations of power confirmed the preaching. The gifts of the Spirit operated freely. The church grew exponentially.

Is it fair to say that the gospel of the modern, western church bears little resemblance to the gospel of the Book of Acts? If you agree, then we urge you to contemplate another question. Should we continue with business as usual or whole-heartedly return to Pentecost?

The truth is, the Bible knows nothing of the watered-down gospel embraced by much of the modern church. The gospel of the Bible is the good news of God's love proclaimed in the power of the Holy Ghost. We don't want to trade that gospel (nor its results) for another gospel – no matter how entertaining or appealing it happens to be. It is our heartfelt prayer that the following scriptures will stir us from our slumber and hasten our return to Pentecost – and to the authentic gospel preached in Pentecostal power.

"In those days came John the Baptist, preaching in the wilderness of Judaea, And saying, Repent ye: for the kingdom of heaven is at hand" (Matthew 3:1-2).

"I indeed baptize you with water unto repentance. But he that cometh after me is mightier than I, whose shoes I am not worthy to bear: he shall baptize you with the Holy Ghost, and with fire" (Matthew 3:11).

"From that time Jesus began to preach, and to say, Repent: for the kingdom of heaven is at hand" (Matthew 4:17).

"And when the day of Pentecost was fully come, they were all with one accord in one place. And suddenly there came a sound from heaven as of a rushing mighty wind, and it filled all the house where they were sitting. And there appeared unto them cloven tongues like as of fire, and it sat upon each of them. And they were all filled with the Holy Ghost, and began to speak with other tongues, as the Spirit gave them utterance" (Acts 2:1-4).

"But Peter, standing up with the eleven, lifted up his voice, and said unto them, Ye men of Judaea, and all ye that dwell at Jerusalem, be this known unto you, and hearken to my words... Now when they heard this (Peter's preaching), they were pricked in their heart (convicted of sin), and said unto Peter and to the rest of the apostles, Men and brethren, what shall we do? Then Peter said unto them, Repent, and be baptized every one of you in the name of Jesus Christ for the remission of sins, and ye shall receive the gift of the Holy Ghost" (Acts 2:14, 37-38).

"And fear came upon every soul: and many wonders and signs were done by the apostles" (Acts 2:43).

"And when they had prayed, the place was shaken where they were assembled together; and they were all filled with the Holy Ghost, and they spake the word of God with boldness... And with great power gave the apostles witness of the resurrection of the Lord Jesus: and great grace was upon them all" (Acts 4:31, 33).

"And great fear (holy reverence) came upon all the church, and upon as many as heard these things. And by the hands of the apostles were many signs and wonders wrought among the people...And believers were the more added to the Lord, multitudes both of men and women. Insomuch that they brought forth the sick into the streets, and laid them on beds and couches, that at the least the shadow of Peter passing by

might overshadow some of them. There came also a multitude out of the cities round about unto Jerusalem, bringing sick folks, and them which were vexed with unclean spirits: and they were healed everyone" (Acts 5:11-12, 14-16).

"Then Philip (a deacon) went down to the city of Samaria, and preached Christ unto them. And the people with one accord gave heed unto those things which Philip spake, hearing and seeing the miracles which he did. For unclean spirits, crying with loud voice, came out of many that were possessed with them: and many taken with palsies, and that were lame, were healed. And there was great joy in that city" (Acts 8:5-8).

The preceding verses were selected from the first eight chapters of Acts. The entire book is filled with such accounts. Space does not permit us to reference all of them. This was normal Christianity in the New Testament: lost souls saved, sick folks healed, demon possessed people delivered. Most modern churches don't even talk about miracles, much less expect one to occur. If a demon manifested in a "seeker-sensitive" service, the pastor would ask ushers to call 911. How far we have fallen! Before it is too late, why don't we try Pentecost one more time?

Chapter Five

We Need Power, Not Programs

The church today, for the most part, is not living in the power of Pentecost. It is stuck between Easter and Pentecost. Believers embrace the Crucifixion and Resurrection, but few live in the power poured out after the Ascension. In the modern church, most believers never climb the stairs to the Upper Room. To them, it is the empty room and, consequently, their lives are devoid of Pentecostal power. Little is known of the power of a life that redeems and lifts above the corruption of the world. We live life on a lower level, beneath the privileges of the redeemed, and fail to rise to the heights of holiness in true Pentecostal power.

The modern church celebrates Easter but not Pentecost. In fact, much of Christendom in the West goes as far as to deny the experience and power of Pentecost. The result is impotence and a corresponding inability to impact society. Without Pentecostal power, we are powerless to influence or move the world toward righteousness.

The church has no message to move the world because

the church has not been moved. Available power has not been appropriated. The message this distracted world will hear must rise up out of vital experience. It must come up out of life – a life which subdues the fleshly nature and triumphs over the world and the devil. Pentecost points to such a life. It fuses potential life and actual life into a living whole. It is not content to know about potential life. It must lay hold of it and pull it into the realm of experience. Knowledge must lead to experience. When the world sees a man who is filled with Pentecostal power, living an abundant spirit-filled life, it will take notice.

We don't need another philosophy of ministry; we don't need more of mans' programs or religious machinery. We need a restoration of Pentecostal power. Pastors in this modern church are infatuated with human programs and machinery. What we need is deeper love for the Holy Spirit. We need to divorce ourselves from the feeble programs of man and commit ourselves anew to humble dependence on the Spirit's power. We need to return to Pentecost. Our problem is that we worship the programs, machinery, and beautiful buildings of religion, but fail to give the Holy Spirit his rightful place in the church. We don't even realize that he has withdrawn to wait outside our beautiful monument to man. He's not coming back inside until a cry rises from within the sanctuary of human souls – a desperate cry which prays, "We need you Holy Spirit. We can't live without you and even if we could, we wouldn't want to."

Pentecost fused power with knowledge and translated doctrine into experience. Christianity is not a religion to be studied and followed. It is a life to be lived – a glorious, resurrected life empowered by Pentecost. At Pentecost the preacher and the preaching became one, the man and the message were carried along by the rivers of living water. The power and preaching of Pentecost brought the church out of the heart and mind of God and planted it in this world. Pentecost produced a new race, a new order. It produced a spiritual family of born again believers who had a new nature. Pentecost makes a man different and sets him apart from the world. Paul said that in Christ we become a new creature (2 Corinthians 5:17). Peter described the newness, the difference, like this:

"But ye are a chosen generation, a royal priesthood, an holy nation, a peculiar people; that ye should shew forth the praises of

him who hath called you out of darkness into his marvelous light"
(1 Peter 2:9).

The church is a nation among the nations. Our government is in heaven. Believers are citizens of another country. We owe our first allegiance to the kingdom of God. We are foreigners, pilgrims passing through this world. But we are here with a mission: a mission to make Jesus known among every tribe, kindred, nation and tongue. We are here to fulfill the Great Commission: an impossible task without the Holy Spirit. Consider the challenge faced by the disciples coming out of the Upper Room. They were charged to preach Jesus Christ as Savior and Lord. The people they preached to believed that Jesus had died. Many of them witnessed his execution. But, they didn't believe the Resurrection. None of them saw it. Peter preached a powerful message to the world outside the Upper Room. But the three thousand who were converted didn't repent just because they heard a powerful message. They were converted because the Holy Spirit dealt with their hearts and convinced them that Peter was preaching the truth. Without the anointing of the Spirit, Peter's words would have fallen to the ground and the disciples would have been driven out of town. The crowd that gathered that day was affected by the same power that transformed the disciples in the Upper Room. The multitude believed because the gospel came not in word only, but in demonstration of the Holy Ghost and power.

Can you imagine what it would have been like to face that hostile crowd with mere human resources? What if there had not been a Pentecost? Would the Church have been born? No. It took power to plant the church in a hostile world. The devil knew the stakes. Jesus, through Holy Ghost filled disciples, was making a move to displace him and replace his kingdom with a new order. The devil realized that this was the beginning of a kingdom that would rule the hearts of men. Unless it was stopped, he knew that the words of the prophet would be fulfilled. *"Of the increase of his government and rule there shall be no end"* (Isaiah 9:7). He knew that if this thing ever got outside of Jerusalem there would be no stopping it. He knew that the glory of the Lord would cover the earth as the water covers the sea.

That's why he summoned all his forces to stop it in its infancy. And he would have succeeded except for one thing: the Holy Ghost had come to take up residence in the hearts of men. The veil of the temple had been rent from top to bottom. The presence of God, his Shekinah glory, had moved from the holy of holies to the hearts of believers. Without this glorious experience, this outpouring of power, the disciples would have never gone forth to challenge the devil's kingdom. They would have remained in hiding behind locked doors, trembling in fear (John 20:19). That fear would have kept their mouths as shut as the doors they were hiding behind. The power of the Holy Ghost made the difference. It transformed fearful hearts into courageous hearts and thrust the disciples out of the Upper Room to confront the kingdom of darkness with boldness and power.

The modern day church must return to Pentecost. Many of us, just like those early disciples, are hiding behind the closed doors of religion. Our faith is so feeble that we shrink in fear of danger and avoid confrontation at any cost. Our pulpits are filled with mice who masquerade as men. They squeak their watered down little sermons because there is no shout in them. When they leave the security of the sanctuary they do their best to blend in with the world in which they live. They don't challenge the evil in society because they have no power to change it. They preach pleasant messages that people want to hear because they don't have enough power to preach what they need to hear. Under the influence of these polite, mild-mannered leaders, the church has become impotent – salt without savor. The church in America has lost its ability to influence the world. The most popular method of evangelism has become friendship with the world. Having lost the power to change the world, the church has created an environment in which the world will feel comfortable. Without the power to change the sinner, we endeavor to entertain him in a "seeker-friendly" atmosphere. The church has become more worldly in order to win the world. It is rare to hear a message like Peter preached on the Day of Pentecost which demands repentance and produces conviction. We need a fresh baptism with the Holy Ghost.

The church was born in Pentecostal power. The church was planted in this world by fervent prayer and strong preaching. If we are to recover what has been lost, we must return to Pentecost. We will not win the world with a watered-down, seeker-friendly gospel. We must have a testimony of power. There must be power in the pulpit. Far too many American preachers have become nothing more than motivational speakers. We need real men of God who

follow the scriptural model and proclaim the whole counsel of
God with boldness and conviction. You may gather a crowd
with entertaining motivational messages, but you will never
produce true disciples of Jesus Christ without proclaiming the
whole counsel of God in the power of the Holy Ghost. There
is no other way to build a New Testament church. We must
have a fresh outpouring of the Holy Ghost.

The church of our day hides behind closed doors of
safety. Modern Christians don't confront the world for fear of
rejection. Their faith is such a feeble thing it wilts at the
thought of rejection. It shrinks in the fear of reproach or
persecution. The faith of the early church did not hide behind
closed doors where a watered-down seeker friendly gospel was
preached. It didn't cry for protection. It courageously
confronted fear and proclaimed the gospel in the power of the
Spirit.

Those early Christians did not seek to make friends
with the world. They marched out with a bold faith to
conquer the world. The church of our day accommodates the
world: creates an atmosphere where the world will feel
comfortable. The church has become more worldly in order

to reach the world. How tragic! The standards have been lowered, the gospel has been diluted, and the power of the Holy Ghost is no longer sought after.

The early church was spontaneous in its expression of the life of Christ. The power of the Holy Ghost flowed freely. There were no well-planned, seeker friendly services. There was no repetitive ritual. They came hungry and thirsty. They came with dependence on the Spirit and with a great desire to see Him move in their midst. There was no order of service, just dependence on the leading of the Spirit. They left excited and filled. They left full of zeal to boldly proclaim the gospel in fullness of power. They didn't conform to the world. They confronted the world and boldly proclaimed, *"God commands all men everywhere to repent."* They left full of life and full of power to manifest that life in the world. We need what they had. We need another Pentecost.

The baptism with the Holy Spirit gave everyone in that upper room power and boldness. It filled them with an inner resource sufficient to face fear and meet the challenge of life. They became *"strong in the Lord and in the power of his might"* through the indwelling of the Holy Spirit. Their inner life was raised to a higher level – a level adequate for the challenges of outer circumstances. Faith opened the doors and propelled them out of the Upper Room to boldly face the mob that had cried for the crucifixion of the Master.

With this exciting example of faith and courage, one is left to wonder why the church today has so neglected the message of Pentecost. We choose man-made programs and reject heaven-sent power. We rely on human wisdom and resources and fail to appropriate heaven's vast supply. We travel familiar roads while the spiritual land of promise and power remains unexplored. Unless we press into those unexplored lands in Pentecostal faith and power, we are destined to wander in the wilderness of mediocrity, contenting ourselves with status-quo, sub-normal Christianity. Power waits, begging to be experienced and used. Why don't we try Pentecost one more time?

Chapter Six

Legalism or Life

We are advocating a return to Pentecost. We are not endorsing many of the doctrines and practices of modern day Pentecostal denominations or churches. We are calling for authentic, credible Christianity which does not insult intelligence. We are promoting holiness, not legalism. A genuine baptism of the Holy Spirit produces enlightenment and life, not ignorance and bondage. Jesus hated the narrow-mindedness of legalistic Pharisees, and He hates the narrow-mindedness of legalistic Pentecostals. As a young believer, I was consumed with desire for the fullness of the Spirit. But I was reluctant to seek it out of fear that it might make me as legalistic as some of the Christians I knew. To this day, I thank God for the good fortune of meeting some Pentecostal believers who were different. I saw both the power and the fruit of the Spirit in their lives. They understood the difference between legalism and holiness.

I came to realize, through months of diligent study on the Holy Spirit, that there was nothing weird about the supernatural. Jesus and the apostles were certainly not infected with the weirdness often practiced in modern churches. They experienced authentic, heaven-sent power and, therefore, did not need the fleshly eruptions we often call manifestations of the Spirit. Real Christianity is shot-through with emotion and feeling because it is filled with life. But the moving of the Spirit does not produce "uncontrollable" displays of flesh and emotion. Joy and excitement can be experienced without the weirdness that too often accompanies what we call the moving of the Spirit. Religious flesh acts stupidly in the presence of power. We must not cheapen the precious move of the Spirit by tolerating confusion and disorder. It is possible to experience the anointing and exercise the gifts of the Spirit without sacrificing order.

"Even so ye, forasmuch as ye are zealous of spiritual gifts, seek that ye may excel to the edifying of the church… I thank my God, I speak with tongues more than ye all: Yet in the church I had rather speak five words with my understanding…than ten thousand words in an unknown tongue. Brethren, be not children in understanding… If therefore the whole church be come together into one place, and all speak with tongues, and there come in those that are unlearned, or unbelievers, will they not say that ye are mad?...For God is not the author of confusion…Wherefore, brethren, covet to prophesy, and forbid not to

54

speak with tongues. Let all things be done decently and in order" (1
Corinthians 14:12, 18-20, 23, 33, 39-40).

The Apostle Paul advocated order, not restricting the manifestation of the Spirit. Churches throughout the western world have failed to understand this. Pastors frustrated with the ignorance that causes religious flesh to get weird in the presence of power, have done the unthinkable. Instead of dealing with the problem, they have placed restrictions on the Spirit. In some cases, the attempts to control His movement caused Him to withdraw. The Holy Spirit will not remain where He is not wanted.

Are you satisfied with the results of restricting the Spirit? Perhaps you have succeeded in creating a comfortable, welcoming atmosphere for "unchurched seekers." Perhaps you have order in a full building. But what have you filled it with? Is the glory still with you, or has a grieving Holy Spirit written "Ichabod" (the glory has departed) over the door to your beautiful building? There is order in a graveyard but I wouldn't want its residents to be members of the church I pastored. A vibrant church filled with life, even if accompanied by occasional chaos and confusion, would be preferable to the quiet order which can be found at the First Church of the Graveyard. It is ludicrous to sacrifice life for order. We must deal with the devil causing the disorder, not restrict the Spirit who brings life.

The powerful preaching of the Book of Acts filled people with supernatural power. The powerless preaching of our day fills buildings with empty people. The Church of the New Testament didn't hire professional musicians and actors to entertain "unchurched seekers." Early believers didn't rely on entertainment, events or programs to attract a crowd. They didn't need to. Jesus was the attraction. Multitudes came from everywhere with expectation and excitement because the real Jesus was among them. They came because the power of God was present to heal and the Holy Ghost was free to move.

The preachers of the early Church were not silk-tongued, motivational speakers. They were men of God with tongues of fire. With deep conviction and passion, they powerfully proclaimed the whole counsel of God. They didn't preach entertaining, humorous sermons in a cozy, seeker-sensitive atmosphere. They charged the gates of hell and challenged the devil wherever they met him. The greatest period of church growth in history was accompanied by sacred fire and supernatural power. The gospel preached and lived in the Book of Acts created excitement everywhere it went. What preacher in his right mind would want to trade that for what we have today?

The Church of the Lord Jesus Christ was born in Pentecostal power. The Church in the Book of Acts shook the world with a revolutionary gospel preached by believers with tongues of fire. That Church is the prototype for the Church of all time. That is the pattern. God has never authorized man to alter it.

We have lost much of what the believers of the New Testament received at Pentecost. We must recover what we have failed to esteem. We must "hunger and thirst for righteousness" to the end that we might once again be filled with life and power. Greater darkness is coming. We need sacred fire and supernatural power to prevail over it. Please, why don't we try Pentecost one more time?

"And when the day of Pentecost was fully come, they were all

with one accord in one place. And suddenly there came a sound from heaven as of a rushing mighty wind, and it filled all the house where they were sitting. And there appeared unto them cloven tongues like as of fire, and it sat upon each of them. And they were all filled with the Holy Ghost, and began to speak with other tongues, as the Spirit gave them utterance" (Acts 2:1-4).

Chapter Seven

Passion and Power

We need preachers who boldly proclaim the truth with certainty and conviction. We need preachers who have been to the Upper Room, who have experienced a personal Pentecost. It is not enough to preach truth. We must preach living truth. We must manifest the life of Christ in our preaching, and in our living. We must live the truth we preach. The world will take notice of such preachers. Somebody will say, "These men are different. Why?" And someone will answer, "They have been with Jesus."

There is a fire burning in the heart of the man who possesses, and preaches, living truth. It is a fire that causes him to preach with passion. Such a man not only possesses truth. He is possessed by truth. He preaches with passion and persuasive power because a fire burns within him – the same fire that Moses saw when a burning bush spoke to him. Our world begs for fired up preachers who burn but don't burn up.

The church lies in spiritual deadness for lack of such men. One need not wonder why an unbelieving world is unmoved and unimpressed. Why should an unbeliever be excited by preaching that flows from a tongue not set on fire by heaven? Why should the world be moved by the preaching of a preacher who himself is not moved by the message he preaches? There was excitement on the Day of Pentecost. There was a testimony of power. The life of Jesus was manifest and multitudes were moved to repentance. That is normal Christianity. The standard was set at the inception of the church. We have drifted far off course. We must cry out for the winds of the Spirit to fill the sails of our souls and propel us forward in Pentecostal power. Without the wind and the fire of the Holy Ghost, we are condemned to live with a sterile, sub-normal brand of Christianity.

Many churches today are weak and anemic. In our weakened state we are in danger of infection from every spiritual germ and virus with which we come in contact. The spiritual immune system of the church is so compromised we seldom discern the presence of danger and deception. When we do, we don't have the strength to stand against them. Nothing but the river of life can cure the ills of the modern church. Without another Pentecost, we are destined to remain trapped in triviality, marooned in the stale marshes of mediocrity. May God help us to realize our condition and move us to rise up in faith to earnestly pray, "Oh, God let the fire fall. Let the winds blow. Let the river flow." Power is waiting for the hungry, for the thirsty. Why don't we try Pentecost one more time?

Has our scientific, western mindset reduced us to sub-normal Christianity? Has it left us trapped somewhere between Easter and Pentecost? Has our refined thinking caused us to shrink back from embracing the supernatural? Are we so governed by the moral reason of the natural mind that normal Christianity – the kind experienced at Pentecost – seems weird to us? Are we in danger of losing the power of Pentecost because we are afraid to embrace the supernatural? We are called to do a supernatural work. When people hear the gospel and are born again they experience a supernatural transformation.

Supernatural work demands supernatural power. New Testament evangelism cannot be done without the power of the Holy Ghost. *"But ye shall receive power after the Holy Ghost has come upon you, and ye shall be witnesses unto me…"* (Acts 1:8). The power evangelism that produced such incredible results on the

Day of Pentecost was a by-product of the baptism of the Holy Spirit.

It would be better to have no concept of God than to have a false one. If we possess moral misconception, we will experience moral misdirection. We will live in confusion and emptiness with no clear purpose for life. The Christian readily understands that the Buddhist, the Hindu, the Muslim, hold a wrong idea of God. They fail to understand that their concept of God rests on a false foundation – that their ideas have been shaped by the teachings and traditions of men and not by the word of God. Has the same tragedy occurred in the sterile church of our day?

God cannot be known or properly perceived by study. He must be revealed. He has revealed Himself in creation, in His word, and in the person of Jesus. But without the illumination of the Holy Spirit we fail to properly understand his revelation. God has revealed himself in the face of Jesus Christ. To look upon his glorious face we must see through the eyes of the Spirit – the Spirit of truth who reveals the Person who is truth. *"Who being the brightness of his glory, and the express image of his person"* (Hebrews 1:3). *"But we all with open face beholding as in a glass the glory of the Lord, are changed into the same image from glory to glory, even as by the Spirit of the Lord"* (2 Corinthians 3:18). *"That the God of our Lord Jesus Christ, the Father of glory, may give unto you the spirit of wisdom and revelation in the knowledge of Him"* (Ephesians 1:17).

Wrong conceptions lead to wrong conclusions. Wrong ideas lead to wrong actions. *"But we speak the wisdom of God in a mystery, even the hidden wisdom which God ordained before the world unto our glory. Which none of the princes of the world knew: for had they known it, they would not have crucified the Lord of glory"* (1 Corinthians 2:7-8). How many atrocities have been committed in the name of religion because someone had a faulty understanding of God? Why did a man like Saul, a lover and seeker of God, persecute, torture and kill the followers of Christ? He held a false idea of God. His moral misconception led to moral misdirection. Much study did not correct his erroneous ideas. Saul became Paul by revelation, not by study. God revealed himself to his servant on the road to Damascus. He was initially blind, frightened, and confused. But when Ananias laid hands on him and said be filled with the Holy Ghost, his eyes were opened. His concept was corrected. He understood in a moment by revelation, what he

63

had failed to understand by years of laborious study (Acts 9:1-18).

God cannot be known through study alone. The Bible is a closed book without the illumination of the Holy Spirit. The life and power of the word of God are locked behind a door that cannot be opened to the natural man. The Holy Spirit holds the key. *"But as it is written, eye hath not seen, nor ear heard, neither have entered into the heart of man, the things which God hath prepared for them that love him. But God hath revealed them unto us by his spirit:..."* (1 Corinthians 2:9-11).

The preacher with a false idea of God fails to preach the whole counsel of God. He emphasizes one truth to the neglect of others. This creates imbalance and misconception which can lead to outright heresy. This is the error of the so-called faith movement. An over emphasis on faith, and an under emphasis on the full body of truth, has created great controversy and confusion in the church. Faith has been reduced to a formula to be used to get blessings from God. The whole message becomes selfish. The gospel is cheapened. The status symbol of faith becomes material prosperity. Covetousness drives those deceived by this so-called word of faith doctrine to treat the great God like some cosmic Santa Claus, who exists to shower them with gifts. Faith is used as a tool to serve man, not God. In fact, carried to the extreme, this moral misconception produces a brand of Christian humanism which displaces God and puts man at the center of the universe. It makes God the servant to faith.

Only revelation by the Spirit can correct this grievous error. The problem, however, is that minds obsessed with a false idea of God are often closed to revelation. A wrong conception often produces a wrong spirit – in this case, an arrogant, unteachable spirit. I was shocked by what a leader in the modern faith movement once told me. I had preached a message on the life of the Apostle Paul, emphasizing the power of faith which produced a victorious attitude, even in the face of great suffering and trial. After the meeting this "faith preacher" came to correct me. He said that if Paul would have possessed a fuller revelation of faith, he would not have suffered so. He went on to explain that we have a greater revelation of faith than the great Apostle because we have the whole Bible, and he had only a portion. I couldn't believe what I was hearing. Such arrogance! Such audacity! I responded by saying; "Sir, the Apostle Paul wrote much of what we know of faith, and what he wrote he received from Jesus in the third heaven."

This is just one of many examples I could give of wrong conceptions leading to a wrong spirit. That preacher was so arrogant he actually believed that his little, imbalanced revelation of faith was greater than that of the Apostle Paul. It is difficult to help such people because they are often narrow in their thinking and not open to instruction. They don't approach the word of God with humility and openness, so the Spirit is not able to give them a clearer revelation. They study the Bible to gain more support for what is already believed, not to be instructed and corrected. Truth which could adjust or correct their faulty understanding does not penetrate. They read it with scales over their eyes. They are blind to anything that contradicts what they have chosen to believe, what they want to believe, but their eyes are wide open to verses which support it. They violate the most basic rules of hermeneutics, lift verses out of context and thus, add to the imbalance and error. Nothing short of a fresh baptism of the Holy Ghost, a fresh saturation with the Spirit of Truth, can lift such souls out of the darkness of false ideas and moral misconceptions.

Another misconception of our day results from an under emphasis on holiness. The most popular preachers in America today preach positive, motivational messages that never confront or convict. Have we traded the passion and power of Pentecostal preaching for entertaining meetings and inspirational talks? There is no precedent to be found from Genesis to Revelation for a preacher who preaches only popular, pleasant sermons which ooze with love. One need only listen to Peter on the Day of Pentecost to know the difference between a real preacher and a motivational speaker. Some will argue and say that Peter's message was to the unbeliever, and that these pleasant, mild-mannered preachers of our day are ministering to edify the church. That argument does not hold water. Both Peter's and Paul's epistles were written to believers for the purpose of edification. But that is only part of the purpose: they are also filled with warning against sin, correction and confrontation. New Testament ministers preach the whole counsel of God.

The over emphasis on love, grace, and mercy has filled the Church with tares who profess to be Christians – professing Christians who have never been born again. They have never been born again because they never repented.

They never repented because they were never convicted of sin. This is the result of the preaching of men who have never been baptized with the real Holy Ghost. A man baptized with the Holy Ghost and fire knows what Jesus said concerning the Spirit of Truth. Such a man preaches the whole counsel of God because he is governed by the Spirit. Therefore, he handles the word of God with integrity and refuses to hold the truth in unrighteousness. Spirit-baptized men know that because God is love, he wants to extend mercy. But, they also know that because God is holy, he must judge sin. They preach law and gospel in balance because they are led and inspired by the Holy Spirit.

The modern, mild-mannered, motivational "preacher" has embraced a false idea, a partial truth, which has resulted in complete error. The error could be corrected by an open-minded reading of just a few passages of scripture. To understand the deception, one need only compare the preaching and lifestyle of these modern men to preachers like Peter and Paul. Their misrepresentation of Christ and the gospel is clearly seen by the believer who is grounded in scripture and filled with the Spirit. Scripture condemns preaching which emphasizes love to the neglect of holiness.

No true preacher of the gospel has the right to preach only positive messages that never deal with sin. Consider what Jesus himself said about the ministry of the Holy Spirit in John 16:8, *"And when he is come, he will reprove the world of sin, of righteousness, and of judgment."*

Preaching inspired by the Holy Ghost deals with the heart and convicts of sin. The Holy Spirit inspires men to righteous living not only because He is holy, but also because He is love. Love holds the truth in righteousness. Love in the heart of a Spirit-filled preacher will move him to preach the whole counsel of God.

The misconceptions of the church growth movement have made a god out of numbers. The pursuit of numerical growth often takes place at the expense of spiritual development. Leaders who glorify bigness have reduced church growth to a mechanical science that leaves little room for the Holy Spirit to move. Grieved and rejected, the Holy Spirit has withdrawn from many churches. Multitudes flock to mega-churches where business continues as usual but God doesn't go there anymore. The sad thing is that he is not even missed.

The seeker friendly, or seeker sensitive, movement has misconceived and misrepresented God. Reverence for a holy God has been replaced with a casual atmosphere where sinners feel at home. This misconception has fashioned a god who is more interested in making sinners comfortable than in getting them converted. This false idea has resulted in a church that will sacrifice truth for relevance, a church that becomes worldly to reach the world. Is it any wonder that our society no longer takes the church or the claims of Christianity seriously? In our quest for relevance we have become so much like the world, it is difficult to see the difference between the believer and the unbeliever. The church has lost its power to influence the world. But the world is exerting great influence on the church.

We have failed to let our light so shine before men that they may see our good works and glorify our Father in heaven. The distinction between saint and sinner is so blurred that the saints feel comfortable in the world and the sinners feel comfortable in the church. How different it was in the early church. The world was an enemy, not a friend. Sinners were confronted with a gospel of power which left no question: to become a Christian meant radical change and departure from the world. Persecution often resulted because the distinction was clear and the demands were strong. There is no evidence of a watered-down gospel or a seeker friendly philosophy in the early church.

John the Baptist came preaching a strong, confrontational message of repentance. Jesus loved sinners but he confronted sin everywhere he went. Beginning with Peter's convicting, confrontational message on the Day of Pentecost, the preachers of the early church thundered out strong messages, fearlessly confronted the darkness, and called sinners to repent and come out from the world. They refused to compromise in the face of persecution and martyrdom. Paul simply stated, *"Yea, all who will live godly in Christ Jesus shall suffer persecution"* (2 Timothy 3:12). These fearless preachers were not comfortable in the world and the world was not comfortable in their churches. They were pilgrims and strangers in the world. They were here on a mission, here to convince others to join them on their journey to a better country. No one misunderstood the message: to go where they were going, a dramatic change was required.

These early disciples changed the world by confronting

it with the most revolutionary message ever heard by mortals: the gospel of the Lord Jesus Christ. They preached the gospel in the power of the Holy Ghost. In just a few years, they carried their revolutionary message to the far corners of the known world. They were consumed with holy fire and passion that few in our day have experienced. Their results confirmed their message. They were men set on fire by heaven, men full of the Holy Ghost. Why don't we try Pentecost one more time?

Chapter Eight

Without the Holy Spirit

While the church in Africa, Asia, and much of Latin America grows exponentially, the church in America languishes and loses members. The 1980's were known as the decade of church growth in America. Countless mega-churches claimed the spotlight throughout that period. But when the dust had settled and the statistics were in, we were shocked to learn that during the decade of church growth the church in America diminished. With all the emphasis on numbers, we did not gain but decreased in proportion to the growth of the population. When the fog lifted, we saw through the hype and realized that most growth was transfer growth. The same people were often counted several times as they hopped from church to church. The percentage of growth by conversion did not keep pace with the growth of the population.

So, what is the difference between the church in America and Africa and Asia? The church in Africa and Asia are experiencing Pentecost. Any preacher who reads reports from around the world knows that the fastest growing segment of Christianity is the Pentecostal church. What is the difference? In Africa and Asia leaders depend on the Holy Spirit, not on human resources or man's programs. They are waiting for the promise of the Father as Jesus instructed, and they are receiving the power of the Holy Ghost just as the early disciples did. They know little of the well-oiled machinery of the church growth movement. They have not compromised the message under the influence of a seeker friendly philosophy. Their gatherings are not as well-planned and organized. They tend to be spontaneous. An air of excitement and an attitude of expectation are present in their meetings. Why? Because the Holy Spirit, not man, is in control. They do not come to a meeting to watch a well-performed drama, to listen to skillfully played music, or to hear a polite preacher deliver a polished sermon. They come to meet God. Because they depend on him, because they expect him to come, the Holy Spirit directs the service, moves among them and stirs their hearts. What is the difference? Pentecost.

A leader from the underground church in China visited the U.S.A. His hosts took him to see mega churches and the headquarters of big ministries. As he prepared to return to

China, someone asked him his impression of the church in America. Thinking he would have been impressed, they were taken back by his response: "I am amazed at how much the church in America is able to do without the Holy Spirit!"

What an indictment. That humble Chinese leader hit the nail on the head. We need no further analysis. Herein lies the problem of the church in America—"without the Holy Spirit:" Without his presence, without his power, without his direction. We have shut him out by choice. We are too impressed with what man can accomplish to give space for the Holy Spirit to work. We are impressed by bigness: big plans and programs, big budgets and buildings. If the church is to recover, we must stop worshipping at the altar of bigness. We must stop glorifying the shallow success of human effort and return to humble dependence on the Holy Spirit. We must become more impressed with the presence and power of the Holy Spirit than with our beautiful places of worship. We pass by the lame man on the steps of our beautiful centers of worship because we are void of power. What is most impressive: sitting down in a beautiful cathedral or saying to the lame man outside, "in the name Jesus Christ of Nazareth rise up and walk?"

What is impressive about sitting down in a beautiful building with a multitude that are not expecting anything out of the ordinary, not expecting the gifts of the Spirit to operate, not expecting his power to be manifest? We should be ashamed of our powerlessness, not impressed by our bigness. It is all empty and vain unless the Spirit of the Holy One comes down.

I once attended a seminar conducted by one of the best known leaders of the church growth, seeker-sensitive movements. He was not nearly so famous in those days and there were only three or four hundred pastors at the seminar. When time allowed, he entertained questions. At one point he stated, "If you want your church to grow, you must realize that you cannot allow verbal manifestations of the gifts of the Holy Spirit in your worship services." He went on to explain that people would be turned off by such supernatural manifestations.

That was his closing comment. I was the only one in the room who took issue with it. You could have heard a pin drop when I asked, "Could you please explain your closing comment in light of the experience of the church in the Book of Acts?" His response made me cringe. It was loaded with human wisdom but void of spiritual understanding. Is it not audacious for a leader to stand before other leaders and say, in essence, that the moving and manifestation of the Holy Spirit will turn people off and cause them not to return for another meeting? Is it not ludicrous for a human being to dictate to the Holy Spirit when and how He can move? His response made me want to shout, "You can have man's methods and programs. Give me the power of Pentecost. You can have your sterile seeker-sensitive religion. Give me the passion and power of Book of Acts Christianity."

The truth is, we need the presence, power, and manifestation of the Holy Spirit as much as those early disciples. We could experience revival if we would trade our worn-out methods for a fresh manifestation of the Holy Ghost. The church was born in Pentecostal power and God intended it to continually function in Pentecostal power. The world in Peter's day surrendered to fire-baptized preaching. We could achieve the same results, if we were truly filled with the same power. Why don't we try Pentecost one more time?

Chapter Nine

What is Missing?

What was missing in Samaria? The eighth chapter of the Book of Acts reports on the great revival that broke out there. After Stephen's martyrdom, great persecution came against the church in Jerusalem. But persecution didn't stop the advance of the gospel. The report of the powerful entrance of the gospel into Samaria is incredible: "*Therefore, they that were scattered abroad went everywhere preaching the word. Philip went down to the city of Samaria, and preached Christ unto them. And the people with one accord gave heed unto those things which Philip spoke, hearing and seeing the miracles which he did. For unclean spirits, crying with loud voices came out of many that were possessed with them: and many taken with palsies, and that were lame, were healed. And there was great joy in that city*" (Acts 8:4-8).

Dare we compare the great revivals and evangelistic crusades of our day to this one in Samaria? Any modern evangelist seeing such results would be ecstatic. It seems that nearly the entire city came out to hear the preaching. Miracles, healings, deliverance from unclean spirits, salvations and baptisms were widespread. An air of excitement permeated the atmosphere, and the result was great joy throughout the city. There was none of the hype, none of the "evangelastic" advertisements, none of the inflation of numbers of many modern crusades.

The whole city had been under the power of an evil sorcerer by the name of Simon. We are told that for a long time he had bewitched them with sorceries. When this powerful sorcerer heard the preaching of Philip, and saw the miracles he performed, he repented and was baptized (Acts 8:9-13). What an incredible move of God. In our day, every Christian magazine, radio and television program would be talking about such a tremendous revival. There would be so much publicity that the evangelist used to lead it would be booked for revivals in mega-churches and invited to appear on the biggest television programs for years to come. He would become a super-star of religion overnight. Not so in Samaria.

They weren't satisfied with the results! Something was missing. Salvations, baptisms, miracles, healings, great deliverances, a whole city stirred: not enough. They had not received the Holy Ghost. The excitement of the revival did not cause them to forget their dependence on the Holy Ghost.

They knew that the results of the revival would be lost unless the Spirit came upon the new believers, as He had come on the believers in the Upper Room on the day of Pentecost.

"Now when the apostles which were at Jerusalem heard that Samaria had received the word of God, they sent unto them Peter and John: who, when they were come down, prayed for them, that they might receive the Holy Ghost. (For as yet he was fallen upon none of them: only they were baptized in the name of the Lord Jesus). Then laid they their hands on them, and they received the Holy Ghost" (Acts 8:14-17).

The revival was not complete until the Holy Ghost fell. How far we have fallen. How we have departed from the New Testament pattern. We hold massive, city-wide crusades and consider them a great success if people come down to the front to pray a prayer to receive Jesus. There are no miracles, healings, or deliverances. The Holy Ghost does not fall. The great evangelist doesn't even pray for the new converts to be baptized in the Holy Ghost. Most leave the same way they came. Few ever become active members of a local church. Without the power of the Holy Ghost operating in their lives, they are quickly overcome by the powers of darkness. They are once again taken captive by the lust of the world. There is no lasting change. The world doesn't even take notice, and even the Christians who attended the meetings soon forget about the "great" revival. Something is missing. We know the statistics. We realize that few of those who walked to the front to pray a little prayer ever become members of a local church. Yet we go on using the same methods in city after city.

The believers in Samaria were wiser than we. They knew, as we know, that something was missing. But they didn't stop short, as we do. The revival continued until the Holy Ghost fell. The difference is clear. The results speak for themselves. Why don't we try Pentecost one more time?

Chapter Ten

Full of Faith and Power

There was something different about the deacons of
the early church. The first negative impression I formed of
Christianity came as a result of the small-spirited deacons in
the church I attended briefly as a child. They were not Christ-
like men. You could find three of them smoking on the
church steps before and after each service. They could never
have served as deacons in the early church, where standards of
holiness were esteemed. Consider the requirements of the
church for their first deacons: *"Wherefore brethren, look ye out
among you seven men of honest report, full of the Holy Ghost and
wisdom, whom we may appoint over this business. But we will give
ourselves continually to prayer, and to the ministry of the word,"* (Acts
6:3-4). In the early church, you couldn't take up on offering or
serve as an usher unless you were filled with the Holy Ghost!

The deacons of the early church did more than count
money, chair committees, and give pastors a hard time. The
first martyr of the church was a Holy-Ghost-filled deacon
named Stephen who preached one of the most powerful
messages of all time, with great boldness, in the face of

persecution and death (Acts 6:8-7:60). Scripture gives more space to this deacon's sermon than it does to Peter's on the Day of Pentecost. Something was different about Stephen. That something is what is missing in much of the modern church in the western world. *"And Stephen, full of faith and power, did great wonders and miracles among the people"* (Acts 6:8). He was full of faith and power because he was full of the Holy Ghost.

God established the pattern in the beginning. The Book of Acts shows us what the church is to be like. The greatest revivals of Christianity, the greatest advance of the church, the greatest missionary movement of all time are seen in the first years of church history. Why can't we go back to the New Testament pattern? Why is it so difficult for us to see the difference, and accept our need for the Holy Ghost? Why don't we trash all the feeble programs of man and return to old fashioned altars to wait for the promise of the Father? Why don't we try Pentecost one more time?

Philip the evangelist was also a Holy-Ghost filled deacon. The great move of God in Samaria took place under his anointed preaching. As we have previously stated, the entire city was impacted. Miracles occurred, healing and deliverance were wide-spread, and conversions were numerous. What was the difference between Philip and most modern day deacons? Power – power that comes from being baptized with the Holy Ghost. He was not only full of wisdom. He was full of life, and when that life flowed out in the power of the Spirit, it was contagious. Church growth resulted.

The early church didn't need a seeker-sensitive philosophy or a church growth program. All those early believers needed was the Holy Ghost. They depended on Him to anoint the word and confirm its preaching with signs following. That is the pattern for church growth. Man-made programs will never be as effective. The greatest period of church growth in history followed the outpouring of the Holy Spirit on the Day of Pentecost. We can't improve on that. Why would we even want to try? Why do we settle for substitutes when we could have the real thing? Why do we settle for programs when we could have the power of the Holy Spirit?

No wonder the early church had such a mighty impact on the first century world. Even its deacons preached with tongues of fire. The gospel advanced in the power of the Spirit. If we want to restore the influence of the church in the world, if we want true revival, we must return to Pentecost.

Yes, there was something different about the deacons of the early church. There was also something different about the members. They were also baptized in the Holy Ghost. To them, the baptism was not optional. It was an absolute necessity. In relentless pursuit, they claimed the promise and prayed until they were filled. Filled with the Spirit, they became invincible men. Persecution could not discourage them. The loss of earthly possessions could not stop them. The members of the early church were consumed with passion, filled with purpose, and anointed with power. Filled with the Spirit, they went out in every direction from Jerusalem and, in a few short years, reached the entire, known world of their day. No other generation has seen the church impact the world as powerfully as that early church. Why? No generation has seen a church so filled with the Holy Ghost. The church that marched out of that Upper Room knew nothing of our modern programs or methods. They had none of the resources we rely on: no buildings, no sound systems, no pianos, guitars, nor organs. But they had the

Spirit in fullness, and that was enough to make kings tremble, empires collapse, and sinners repent.

There is no secret to their success. Nothing is hidden. The difference between them and us is clear. *"They were all baptized in the Holy Ghost."* The members of the early church didn't go to meetings to be entertained. They went to enter in and experience the moving of the Spirit in their midst. They were not spectators. They went to meetings to participate. They went expecting God to move in power and manifest His glory. They knew nothing of sterile, seeker-friendly gatherings. There was expectation and excitement when they assembled. They knew nothing of our modern day, non-confrontational preaching. They listened to anointed, Holy Ghost-filled preachers who proclaimed the whole counsel of God. Is it any wonder they were different than the majority of modern day, spoon-fed, barely-alive believers?

The members of the early church came to meetings excited, expecting to participate because the Spirit of God was active in their lives. They had an up-to-date testimony. They came into a meeting with openness of heart, yielded to the Holy Spirit, available should He want to use them to minister in the gifts of the Spirit, or in some other way. They experienced true body ministry. There may have been some confusion in the Corinthian church, which Paul had to straighten out, but it is certain they didn't have something the modern church often does: boredom. There was excitement; things were stirred up because the Spirit of God was moving.

It is much more exciting to participate in something that is alive, than to be a spectator who sits down to be entertained among the spiritually dead. Man's entertaining programs are a cheap substitute for the presence of Jesus and the life of the Spirit.

Many have referred to the confusion in the Corinthian church when arguing against the manifestation of the gifts of the Spirit. It is a foolish argument. Paul was careful in his correction and instruction to the Corinthian believers. He took nothing away from the Holy Spirit. He wanted the gifts to operate. He closes 1 Corinthians 14 by saying that we should "covet to prophesy" and that we should "forbid not to speak in tongues." Paul wanted the gifts to operate. He wanted the believers to participate. His instruction was to move in the gifts, but do so in an orderly manner.

The gifts of the Spirit created excitement in the early church. The absence of the gifts of the Spirit in the modern church has led to boredom and apathy. The tragedy is that, in the absence of the gifts, modern-day Christians have not gone to the altar to seek a fresh baptism of the Holy Ghost. In many churches, (even our Pentecostal churches) they couldn't find an altar if they wanted one. Instead of seeking a fresh baptism of the Holy Ghost, we have accepted cheap substitutes in a religious system ruled by man. Some of the most famous, most popular preachers of our day are nothing more than soul-masters who know how to manipulate a crowd. With lighting, music, and special effects, they create an artificial atmosphere and call it the anointing. Sadly, bored-believers who are not filled with the Holy Ghost can't discern the difference.

In an earlier chapter I mentioned that I once attended a church growth conference conducted by one of the best known preachers in America today. He wasn't as famous then and there were only about five-hundred in attendance. I was appalled at some of the things he said. He is one of the gurus of the so-called seeker-sensitive or seeker-friendly movement.

Basically, he was teaching that crowd of pastors that if they wanted their churches to grow they would have to design services where un-churched people (you can never call them lost or you might offend them) would feel comfortable. I surmised that to adopt his philosophy I need only shorten my sermon, water-down my message, never preach against sin, nor say anything that would challenge or convict. There is just one problem with the church growth message propagated by the "gurus" of the seeker-sensitive movement: their message bears no resemblance to the message preached in the Book of Acts, no resemblance to the message preached during the greatest period of growth in church history. Shouldn't we at least take another look at Pentecost?

Chapter Eleven

Come Up Higher

It's time to understand that the Holy Spirit is given for more than just our personal blessing. We must move from blessing to obedience. There is much more to the Baptism in the Holy Spirit than we realize. God has so much more to give us. He is always saying come up higher, wade in deeper – I have more for you!

I would like to raise four questions in this chapter: "Why do you need the Baptism in the Holy Spirit? Are you full of the Holy Spirit? Are you thirsty? Do you want to receive?"

First of all, why do we need the Baptism in the Holy Spirit? There are many reasons. The Holy Spirit produces the character of Jesus that causes us to die to our flesh; love is shed abroad in our hearts by the Holy Spirit. To be baptized by the Holy Spirit is to be baptized in love. Love is the greatest need of the human heart, and the Holy Spirit is the Spirit of love.

We need the fire of God in our souls. This holy fire consumes what is bad and purifies what is left. It purges and refines. Some people misunderstand the refining fire of the Holy Spirit, and are therefore not perfected in holiness. We must yield to this purifying process in order to mature in the Lord. The baptism puts the fire in you and you in the fire. We must not fear the fire. It is possible to meet Jesus there and emerge purified from the flames without the smell of smoke on you (Daniel 3:21-27).

The Spirit helps us in our prayer life. It is so wonderful to be able to pray in a language that goes beyond our human understanding. There are times when the problems and needs of the world overwhelm me. I don't know what to pray in English. How precious it is to pray in the Spirit and know that He has no limits. Our prayer can be touching a poor woman in Africa or a persecuted brother in China. It could also be for ourselves. The Spirit prays through us – for us.

Another reason we need the Baptism in the Holy Spirit is righteousness, peace, and joy. The Holy Spirit helps us live righteous lives, produces peace in our hearts and gives us joy. God never intended for man to get bound up with dead, dry tradition. God is full of joy and excitement. He wants us to experience "joy unspeakable and full of glory." For many Christians it is "trials unbearable and full of misery." Go to many churches and if you breathe too loudly everyone will do a double-take. Where did we ever get the idea that God doesn't want us to be joyful in church? What better place to get excited and do a little shouting? If you can't stand a little joyful noise, you will never make it in heaven. Heaven is going to be a noisy place (Revelation 5:19-13). The Bible is a noisy book. It is filled with trumpet blowing, hand clapping and shouting. God has always loved the praises of His people. I can't help becoming emotional about Jesus! Religion doesn't have any emotion. I don't want any religion. I have a relationship: a relationship with Jesus – the most exciting person in the universe. Now that's reason to shout and sing. It is no wonder many churches are not reaching the younger generation. Youth must have an outlet for their emotions. Youth have not turned away from Jesus – they have turned away from unemotional, dead, dry religion.

The Holy Spirit reveals the truth to us. In a day of so many cults and false religions we certainly need the Holy Spirit to lead us into all truth. The word of God opens up – comes alive – to us after we are baptized in the Holy Spirit.

The Holy Spirit is the precious comforter. We all have times when we need to be comforted. Nothing compares to the compassion and comfort of the Holy Spirit. He is sensitive to and concerned about our needs. He knows how to heal our hurts.

The Holy Spirit gives us power! We need the power of God to do the work of God. Too many churches are running on man's machinery, not God's power. The Holy Spirit not only gives us power to witness – He gives us power to live a victorious life. Through the Holy Spirit we can have victory even in the midst of trying circumstances. Immediately after Jesus received the blessing of the baptism, He was driven by the Spirit into the wilderness. What happened there? He was tempted of the devil. He waged spiritual warfare. He won the battle in the power of the Spirit. You may find yourself in the greatest spiritual battle of your life after receiving the Baptism in the Holy Spirit – but now you have a greater power with which to fight. Acts 1:8 says specifically that we will receive power to be witnesses. What a wonderful privilege to be called and empowered by God to go forth to share the glorious gospel. As Christians, the power of God is available to us. It remains for us to reach out and receive it by faith.

Secondly, are you full of the Holy Spirit? I didn't ask if you had a "once upon a time" experience when you spoke in tongues. Are you full of the Holy Spirit now? I know a lot of people who experienced the Baptism of the Holy Spirit some time ago – but they are not full of the Spirit now. Some people are too full of self to be filled with the Spirit. Others are too full of love for the world to be filled with the Spirit. If your heart is not surrendered to God, you are not full of the Holy Spirit. Being full of the Holy Spirit makes you do more than speak in tongues, clap your hands and say "Praise the Lord" once in a while. It will revolutionize and revitalize your life.

If you want to experience the fullness of the Spirit, surrender yourself fully to God. Someone has said, "It is not just a question of how much of the Holy Spirit I have but how much of me does He have?"

There was tremendous excitement around Jesus. Wherever He went miracles occurred. Why? He was given over completely to the Father. He stayed full of the Holy Spirit. Wherever He went you could hear people saying, "Look. It's Jesus coming! Look, He's touching the lame man – he's walking! There's a blind man coming – now he can see!"

Thirdly I want to ask, are you thirsty? Sometimes life is like a big desert. We desperately need a drink of the living water of God's Spirit. There is a river that is constantly flowing out from the throne of God (Psalm 46:4; Revelation 22:1). We need to plunge into that river and stay in its flow. We need to drink in the Spirit and then release it to flow out from us. It should be like a well bubbling up inside and springing forth – going out of us to bless others. Did you ever notice what happens to a stream when it stops flowing? It becomes a stagnant pool. We must release the Spirit to flow out from us, if we desire God to pour more into us. God wants to quench our thirst with living water. "*In the last day, that great day of the feast, Jesus stood and cried, saying, if any man thirst, let him come unto me and drink*" (John 7:37).

Finally, do you want to receive? Yes, but…But what? Give me one good reason why you shouldn't open up and receive all that God has for you? He asked the widow in 2

Kings 4, "*What do you want me to do for you?*" He is asking you the same thing. He wants to bless you (Luke 11:13). How long will you be slack to enter in and receive your inheritance (Joshua 18:3)? The blessings are there – God has already provided them. It's up to you to exercise faith and receive them. The first generation of the children of Israel got right to the edge of the Promised Land. They could see it, smell it. It was right in their grasp. It was so close – they were right on the edge – but they didn't enter in. Don't be like them! Reach out and receive what God has for you. You know you need it. I believe you want it. If you are hungry and thirsty, why not pursue it? Why not come up higher into the fullness of the Spirit? Let's try Pentecost one more time.

Chapter Twelve

Spirit-Empowered Ministry

Here is the key to power. Here is the pattern for ministry: "*How God anointed Jesus of Nazareth with the Holy Ghost and with power; who went about doing good, and healing all that were oppressed of the devil, for God was with him*" (Acts 10:38).

First came the anointing and the power; then came the ministry. Jesus, throughout His earthly life and ministry, lived in absolute dependence on the Holy Spirit. He emptied himself (Philippians 2:6-8) that He might be filled with all the fullness of God (Colossians 2:9). Herein lies the secret of His obedience, His effectiveness, and His power: He depended fully on the Holy Spirit. Every word He spoke, every action He took, was directed by the Spirit.

Jesus did not come to please Himself, serve Himself, nor to do His own will. He came to please God, serve God and man, and do the will of God. "*I delight to do thy will O God, yea, thy law is within my heart*" (Psalm 40:8). He was emptied of self, filled with the Spirit, and poured out in service. He gave all the credit to the Spirit of God which filled and anointed

Him. Every healing He performed, every miracle He demonstrated, every demon He cast out was by the power of the Spirit. He was quick to declare *"I do nothing of myself"* (John 8:28-29). When He raised Lazarus from the dead, He first addressed the Father (John 11:41-43), then He commanded Lazarus to come forth. He was careful that in every demonstration of authority and power, the glory should go to God.

His was a life of absolute trust and complete dependence on the Father. He relied totally on the Holy Spirit to reveal the Father's will, and then to empower Him to perform it.

"For I have not spoken of myself; but the Father which sent me, he gave me a commandment, what I should say, and what I should speak. And I know that his commandment is life everlasting: whatsoever I speak therefore, even as the Father said unto me, so I speak" (John 12:49-50).

How could someone live in such intimate communion with the Father? Only by the Spirit. Jesus lived every day, every moment, in perfect fellowship with and perfect dependence upon the Holy Spirit. To hear the Son of Man speak was to hear the voice of the Spirit. To see the Son of Man act was to see the power of the Spirit manifest.

"For I have given unto them the words which thou gavest me; and they have received them, and have known surely that I come out from thee, and they have believed that thou didst send me" (John 17:8).

To see Jesus was to see the Father. To hear Jesus was to hear the voice of God. Why? Because He so emptied Himself that, by the Spirit, the God head was fully expressed through Him.

Jesus began His ministry with a declaration of dependence upon the Holy Spirit. After forty days of fasting and fighting the devil, Jesus prevailed and returned to Nazareth where He began His public ministry with these words:

"The Spirit of the Lord is upon me, because he hath anointed me to preach the gospel to the poor; he hath sent me to heal the brokenhearted; to preach deliverance to the captives; and recovering of sight to the blind; to set at liberty them that are bruised; to preach the

acceptable year of the Lord" (Luke 4:18-19).

Jesus began His public ministry in the power of the Spirit, and He carried out and ultimately fulfilled His ministry in that same power. Hanging on the cross, He was able to look with eyes of faith to see the spoiling of Satan's kingdom. At that moment He cried, *"It is finished."* He was able to make that statement because, from beginning to end, He lived in absolute dependence on the Holy Spirit.

He laid down His life in faith trusting that the same Spirit which had anointed Him would bring Him back from the dead. He was not disappointed:

"Concerning his Son Jesus Christ, our Lord, which was made of the seed of David according to the flesh; and declared to be the Son of God with power, according to the spirit of holiness, by the resurrection from the dead" (Romans 1:3-4).

Hear the testimony of John the Baptist when he baptized Jesus in the Jordan River: *"And John bear record saying; I saw the Spirit descending from heaven like a dove, and it abode upon him. And I knew him not; but he that sent me to baptize with water, the same said unto me; upon whom thou shalt see the Spirit descending and remaining on him, the same is he which baptizeth with the Holy Ghost"* (John 1:32-33). *"John answered saying unto them all, I indeed baptize you with water, but one mightier than I cometh…he shall baptize you with the Holy Ghost and fire"* (Luke 3:16). *"And Jesus being full of the Holy Ghost returned from Jordan, and was led by the Spirit into the wilderness"* (Luke 4:1).

Before Jesus went to fight the devil, He was filled with the Holy Ghost. Before He began His public ministry, He was filled with the Holy Ghost. From that day forward, in every confrontation with the kingdom of darkness, Jesus depended on the power of the Holy Ghost. From that day forward, whenever He was challenged by human need, Jesus depended on the power of the Holy Ghost. He lived by the Spirit. He walked in the Spirit. He prayed in the Spirit. He ministered in the Spirit. Every miracle performed, every healing administered, every demon cast out, was by the power of the Spirit. There is no question, no room for argument on this point. By His own testimony, we know that of Himself He did nothing. In all things, He depended fully on the Holy Ghost. How much more should we?

Not only did Jesus live by the Spirit and minister in the Spirit, He taught much about our need for the Spirit. Early in His ministry we find Him instructing His disciples to ask for the Holy Spirit:

"...Ask and it shall be given you; Seek and ye shall find; Knock and the door shall be opened unto you...If ye then being evil, know how to give good gifts unto your children, how much more shall your heavenly Father give the Holy Spirit to them that ask him" (Luke 11:9,13).

"In the last day, that great day of the feast, Jesus stood and cried saying, 'If any man thirst, let him come unto me and drink. He that believeth on me, as the scriptures hath said, and out of his belly shall flow rivers of living water': But this spake he of the Spirit which they that believe on him should receive" (John 7:37-39).

So, we can clearly see that He began His ministry in the Spirit, He carried out His ministry in the power of the Spirit, and throughout His ministry He taught His disciples concerning their need for the Spirit (John 16:5-16).

He was still stressing their need for the Holy Spirit, just before He ascended. Don't let the importance of this fact escape you: Jesus placed great importance on the baptism with the Holy Ghost. His final words to His disciples were to wait for the coming of the Spirit:

"And behold I send the promise of my Father upon you, but tarry ye in Jerusalem, until ye be endued with power from on high" (Luke 24:49).

Jesus had faith to release His ministry to the disciples because He trusted in the Holy Spirit. He knew that the ministry of the Spirit through His life would now be multiplied in the lives of many disciples.

"And being assembled together with them, commanded them that they should not depart from Jerusalem but wait for the promise of the Father…For John truly baptized with water; but ye shall be baptized with the Holy Ghost, not many days hence…But ye shall receive power, after that the Holy Ghost is come upon you…And they were all filled with the Holy Ghost, and began to speak with other tongues as the Spirit gave them utterance" (Acts 1:4-5,8; 2:4).

They waited as He commanded, they received as He promised, and they went out preaching in power as He commissioned them to do. Mark records the results: *"And they went forth and preached everywhere, the Lord working with them, and confirming the word with signs following"* (Mark 16:20).

From His conception to His ascension, Jesus Christ depended on the Holy Ghost. In Him, He lived and moved and had His being. Every message He preached, every miracle He performed, were by the power of the Spirit. He was conceived by the Holy Ghost, kept by the Holy Ghost, empowered by the Holy Ghost, and raised from the dead by the Holy Ghost. Even in His sacrificial death we see His dependence on the Spirit. Hebrews 9:14 tells us that Jesus *"through the eternal spirit offered himself to God."*

Never has a life been lived in greater dependence on the Spirit. May the same Spirit who conceived and kept, guided and empowered Jesus Christ our Lord, give us wisdom to follow His example. May the pattern of Holy Spirit inspired, Holy Spirit anointed ministry be made clear. May we empty ourselves and cry with utmost sincerity and humility, "Holy Spirit we need you."

Jesus depended on the power of the Holy Ghost. He taught His disciples to do the same. The church born on the Day of Pentecost was a Holy-Ghost filled church. The church that exploded in every direction, as recorded in the Book of Acts, was a Holy Ghost-filled church. If Jesus needed the power of the Holy Ghost, if the early disciples needed the power of the Holy Ghost, if the early church needed the power of the Holy Ghost, how much more do we? Why don't we try Pentecost one more time?

Chapter Thirteen

The Other Side of Calvary

Man needs power. God gives power. He gives it to men qualified to receive it. What are the qualifications? Humility and hunger, faith and obedience. *"For the eyes of the Lord run to and fro throughout the whole earth to show himself strong in the behalf of them whose heart is perfect toward him"* (2 Chronicles 16:9). When God's strength is revealed His power is released. He ever searches for men whom He can trust with His power.

Man needs power, wants power, and often lusts for power. In his lust, he reaches for power unlawfully. That was the devil's demise, and men in their lust and pride make the same mistake.

Much of the bloodshed and war that mark human history are the result of the selfish pursuit of power. The kingdoms of this world are erected on the lust for power. Many men, once godly, have fallen down at this point. Satan knew well man's lust for power. That is why he tempted Jesus with the kingdoms of the world.

But Jesus was not like the "first Adam." He rejected

the devil's offer and chose God's will. He refused to take power unlawfully and chose rather to wait humbly before God, until it was given. In God's economy, power is not something to be taken. It is a gift to be received.

Satan's path to power is by usurping and the asserting of self. God's way to power is by humility and the surrendering of self. Legitimate power is given for service. It is received in greatest measure on the other side of sacrifice. It was on the other side of Calvary that Jesus said "*All power is given unto me in heaven and in earth*" (Matthew 28:18). Let us be quick to remember that Pentecost followed Calvary. And let us note carefully that the power of Pentecost must be exercised in the spirit of Calvary. By this power we rule over the forces of darkness, but with this same power we serve men. Power is given for service.

"*Ye know that the princes of the Gentiles exercise dominion over them, and they that are great exercise authority upon them. But it shall not be so among you: but whosoever will be great among you, let him be your minister; and whosoever will be chief among you, let him be your servant*" (Matthew 20:25-27).

Man is destined for dominion. God created him so: *"let him have dominion"* (Genesis 1:26). God put man in the Garden of Eden and breathed dominion into his soul. He gave him authority, the right to rule. He gave him power, and the authority to exercise that power. But Adam was unwilling to live in dependence upon God. By his desire for self-exaltation, self-realization, he was tempted to act independently of God. His rebellion was his ruin. He lost his dominion, his authority, and the power that enabled him to exercise dominion. Dominion does not exist without authority and authority is useless without power. Without power, authority, even if it is possessed, cannot be exercised.

Adam lost power and authority when he sank in surrender to sin. Jesus came to restore what Adam lost. His final promise to the men who followed Him was the restoration of power. He had already given them authority to operate in His name. Now He promises to give them power to exercise that authority.

"And behold I send the promise of my Father upon you; but tarry ye in the city of Jerusalem until ye be endued with power from on high" (Luke 24:49). *"But ye shall receive power after that the Holy*

Ghost is come upon you…" (Acts 1:8).

The last promise Jesus gave His disciples was the promise of power. In the first chapter of Acts, Luke records the words of Jesus concerning the baptism with the Holy Ghost and the reception of power. We see the promise fulfilled, and we witness the immediate effects of the power poured out on the disciples in chapter two. Fearful Peter is instantly transformed into a courageous preacher and three thousand souls are swept into the kingdom of God in the first meeting of the early church.

The record is clear. The church was born in Pentecostal power. The need of the modern church is also clear: the same power that filled that Upper Room on the Day of Pentecost. Jesus intended that the church born in Pentecostal power continue to operate in that same power throughout the ages. The modern church which has substituted man's programs for God's power will never triumph over the powers of darkness. Nothing can replace Pentecost. Nothing can substitute for the Baptism of the Holy Ghost.

Power is a byproduct of the Baptism with the Holy Ghost. We need the power. We need Him more. The power comes with the Person. We must seek the Giver, not just the gift. The gift is part of the package. The power is found in the presence of the Person. We miss the mark if we seek only the power of the Spirit. What we need is the Spirit of power. Let us seek the Giver, not the gift, knowing that to receive the Giver is to receive the gift.

The will of God cannot be realized in the strength of the flesh. The work of God can only be accomplished in the power of the Spirit. Man may erect great cathedrals and fill them with worshippers without attracting God's attention. Men may be impressed by the buildings, the programs, and the hustle and bustle of religious activity. God is not. He looks for life. Where the Spirit is at work, the life of Christ will be manifest, the power of God will be released, and the devil will be disturbed.

The modern church is often so bankrupt of life the devil can sit in the front row and never have an uncomfortable moment. He does not fear religion. He does not fear the arm of the flesh. But he flees from the presence of the Holy One.

The devil abides in darkness and death. He is tormented by light and life. He fears the fire and power of Pentecost. He has no quarrel with religion. His conflict is with life. That is why he fears Pentecost. Where the Spirit of power is poured out, the life of Jesus is manifest.

Why would we ever want a substitute for the Holy Spirit? Why would we lean on the arm of flesh? Why would we trust in worldly, natural resources when the supernatural resources of heaven are available to us? We are here to do a supernatural work. We are engaged in warfare with a supernatural enemy. The work must be waged in the power of the Spirit. How foolish we are to take up this work and enter this warfare with carnal resources and weapons. God meant it when he said, *"It is not by might, nor by power, but by my Spirit, saith the Lord"* (Zechariah 4:6). Jesus meant it when He said, *"It is the Spirit that quickeneth, the flesh profiteth nothing: the words that I speak unto you, they are spirit and they are life"* (John 6:63). Paul knew what he was talking about when he proclaimed, *"For the weapons of our warfare are not carnal, but mighty through God to the pulling down of strongholds"* (2 Corinthians 10:4). The Spirit's power, weapons, and life: by these shall we prevail over the kingdom of darkness; by these shall we establish the church and advance the cause of Christ.

We are not deceived. We know something is missing. It is not difficult to see the difference between the church of the Book of Acts and the church of our day. That early church was filled with Holy Ghost power. The atmosphere was charged with the electricity of resurrection life. With great power, the apostles preached the gospel, and their gospel was confirmed with signs following. The lame walked, the deaf heard, the blind received their sight. Sick people were healed by Peter's passing shadow. Demons fled at the word of those first preachers. Disease departed at their command. Convicted sinners repented and cried out for mercy. Churches were multiplied, the kingdom of God advanced. Why? The early church was a Pentecostal church, a church baptized in the Holy Ghost.

The contrast is clear. The problem is evident. We lack power. We have departed from Pentecost. We don't see what that early church saw because of the poverty of our spiritual life. The power Jesus promised is sadly lacking in the church today. The majority of Pentecostal churches are Pentecostal in name only. We have lost the fire, the life, the power of the

Spirit. We will never see true revival without them. There is no substitute for the Holy Ghost. Why don't we try Pentecost one more time?

Chapter Fourteen

A Tongue of Fire

The pen is mightier than the sword. The mouth is mightier than the pen. Nothing can move men as can a tongue set on fire by heaven. The church advances with a tongue of fire. Peter rose up out of the fear that caused him to deny Jesus with a tongue of fire. The first sermon of the church of the Lord Jesus Christ was delivered by a Pentecostal preacher whose tongue was set on fire by heaven. A spirit of conviction and holy fear swept over the crowd, men cried out *"What must we do to be saved,"* and the church exploded in the power of Pentecost. Why should we settle for less today?

Throughout history, the church has advanced with a tongue of fire. Where there is no fire, there is no passion, power, or purity. Where there is no fire, love grows cold and vibrant Christianity becomes stale religion. Revivals of religion are always accompanied by fire. The fire prepares the way for the power of God. The power of the Holy Ghost falls on vessels purified by fire. The dross must be burned up. The vessel must be purged; the heart must be made pure to prepare the way for the Spirit of the Holy One to come down. Key events in Bible history are marked by fire. Holy fire attracted Moses to a bush that burned but was not consumed (Exodus 3). That holy fire never left Moses. It stayed with him through the wilderness. It met him again on Mt. Sinai when he received the Law and the pattern for the Tabernacle. The fire of God's presence, symbolized by the candlestick before the veil of the holy of holies, burned continually in the Tabernacle. From the moment of his encounter with God at the burning bush, Moses moved with the fire. His heart was hot with holy purpose. God's voice, speaking out of the holy fire burning in his heart, devastated the most powerful empire on earth and delivered an entire nation.

Elijah's prayers were fueled with the fervor of holy fire. He called on the God who answered by fire and, in one day, destroyed eight-hundred fifty false prophets, and brought a backslidden nation back to God. Revival followed the fire and the heavens were opened over Israel once again (1 Kings 18).

The Old Testament ends with reference to a fire that will consume the wicked (Malachi 4). The New Testament begins with reference to a holy, purifying fire that comes with the Baptism of the Holy Ghost (Matthew 3:11). The church was birthed on the Day of Pentecost with a baptism of power and fire (Acts 2:1-4). Paul exhorts believers to *"serve God acceptably with reverence and godly fear: For our God is a consuming fire"* (Hebrews 12:28-29). Peter tells us that on the Day of the Lord *"the heavens being on fire shall be dissolved, and the elements shall melt with fervent heat…the earth also and the works that are therein shall be burned up"* (2 Peter 3:10,12).

Peter, like Paul, when contemplating this consuming fire, exhorts God's people to live holy lives: *"Seeing then that all these things shall be dissolved, what manner of persons ought ye to be in all holy conversation and godliness"* (2 Peter 3:11).

The church was born in the presence of holy fire. It advances with a tongue of fire. Revivals of religion are preceded by and accompanied with fire. The earth and the heavens are consumed with holy fire. *"New heavens and a new earth, wherein dwelleth righteousness"* follow the purifying fire that does away with the former heavens and earth (2 Peter 3:13). Christianity from start to finish is a religion of fire. Therefore, Christianity from start to finish demands holiness, for nothing unholy can survive holy fire. What manner of persons ought we to be? Holy living requires power. Shouldn't we try Pentecost one more time?

Chapter Fifteen

Fresh Fire

Revival comes with fire. It continues with fire. The flames of spiritual devotion are fanned by the wind of true heaven-sent revival. Counterfeit revivals stir the emotions but never deepen spiritual devotion. In the modern church, men without the Holy Spirit kindle their own fire. Sadly, many modern Christians are not able to discern between the true and false. The brass looks beautiful to those who have never seen the gold. The devil, knowing that there can be no real power without fire, erects altars attended by priests bearing false fire. The Bible calls it "strange fire" (Leviticus 10:1; Numbers 26:61).

Strange fire, to the natural eye, has the appearance of the genuine. The difference is seen in the effects. It stirs the emotions but, unlike true Pentecostal fire, it lacks power to move the spirit or purify the heart. The wide-spread presence of this counterfeit fire in the modern church explains the lack of reverence and moral conviction among the people of God. It also explains the loss of impact and influence on the world around us. A church which has lost its fire is of no more use than salt that has lost its savor.

The modern church does not discern the gravity of her fireless condition. Jesus tells us clearly how he feels about a church that, through compromise, neglect, or sin, has lost its fervor. *"So then because thou art lukewarm and neither cold not hot, I will spew thee out of my mouth"* (Revelation 3:16). A church that has lost its fire is filled with Christians who have lost their savor. Consider again what Jesus said in Matthew 5:13: *"We are the salt of the earth; but if the salt has lost its savor, wherewith shall it be salted? It is thenceforth good for nothing, but to be cast out, and to be trodden under foot of men."*

Is this not what is happening to the modern church in America and Europe? The world laughs and tramples truth under foot because so many of our leaders have held the truth in unrighteousness. Truth is not esteemed because men who are not consumed with the spirit of truth preach it without fire. Not having love for the truth, they handle it unrighteously. They add to it and take away from it; they water it down and disfigure it; they twist and pervert it. Worst of all, they do not love the truth, and for this reason more than any other, a watching world turns away from the truth that could save it.

Throughout church history God has found men who not only lived the truth they preached, but were willing to die for it. Such men are yet among us but in ever diminishing numbers. Nothing less than fire from heaven can correct this malady. In the absence of the purifying fire of Pentecost, the truth will continue to be mishandled, maligned, and misrepresented.

The world cannot see the truth because it sees those who claim to preach it. The majority are not rejecting the message but the messenger. The dichotomy that exists between preaching and living is appalling. Preachers, once highly respected in American society, are now looked upon with disdain once reserved for loan sharks and dishonest lawyers. Preachers are no longer believed or trusted by the majority – inside or outside the church. Famous leaders being exposed for adultery and scandals involving money have become so commonplace we are no longer shocked when we hear that another one of the "mighty has fallen."

A lukewarm church tolerates hypocrites in her pulpits

with little thought of the tragedy caused by such gross misrepresentation of truth. A watching world, because of its disdain of the messenger, tramples truth underfoot and continues its descent into deeper darkness. Isaiah's description of a world in darkness, and a "church" without power to influence that world, accurately portrays the present moral crisis. God, speaking through His prophet, begins Isaiah 59 by clearly telling His people the root cause of all the trouble: *"Your iniquities have separated between you and your God, and your sins have hid his face form you, that he would not hear"* (Isaiah 59:2). After a long list of evils found among God's people, the prophet laments that *"truth has fallen in the street"* (v.16). Truth is trodden under foot, valued no more than salt that has lost its savor. How long will we let it lie there? How long will we tolerate hypocritical preachers who offer strange fire on our altars? How long will we be content to live without revival?

The church was born in Pentecostal power accompanied by fire from heaven. The church Jesus comes back for will be filled with the same Pentecostal power and burning with the same Pentecostal fire. He will come for a bride that "has made herself ready," a bride "without spot or blemish," a bride that has been purified by fire.

Nothing less than the purifying fire of Pentecost can get the church ready for the visitation we so desperately need. If we repent for our failure to love and live the truth, the fire will fall again. *"And the Redeemer shall come to Zion, and unto them that turn from transgression in Jacob"* (Isaiah 59:20). *"As many as I love, I rebuke and chasten: be zealous therefore, and repent"* (Revelation 3:19). We need power. We need purity. The power will come with His presence. The purity will come with His fire. We need a fresh baptism with the Holy Ghost and fire.

Nothing else will do. Nothing less can lift us. Why don't' we try Pentecost one more time?

Chapter Sixteen

Fire on the Altar

For too long, we Pentecostals have lamented the absence of fire without fervently praying for a fresh baptism of fire. To lament lack of fire, without praying for fire, is as futile as preaching against darkness without turning on the light. We somehow feel a bit more spiritual for having recognized the problem, but both approaches produce the same thing: nothing. The darkness will never leave until the light drives it away. Fire will not fall where fervent prayer is not offered. Fire does not fall on empty altars. Fire follows fervent prayer as surely as daylight follows the night. It was so at Pentecost, and it has been so in every revival since.

God is looking for empty vessels: empty vessels who pray for fire and fullness. Men of power and fire have always been praying men. When I think of praying men, three always come to mind: Elijah, John the Baptist, and Jesus. All were men who spent long periods in seclusion, away from the crowds, waiting, listening, and communing with God in prayer. When they returned to public ministry it was always with Holy Ghost power and a tongue of fire. Such men touch heaven, shake hell, and move the world. Someone has said of Jesus, "He moved from one place of prayer to another and did miracles in between."

"…he went out into a mountain to pray, and continued all night in prayer to God" (Luke 6:12).

"And in the morning, rising up a great while before day, he went out, and departed into a solitary place, and there prayed" (Mark 1:35).

The demands human need placed on one as compassionate as Jesus required power. They were more than could be met with natural resources. Even Jesus had to depend on heaven for zeal to minister and power to work. The importance He placed on prayer is underscored by His habit of regularly withdrawing from the multitudes to spend time alone with God.

"But so much the more went there a fame abroad of him; and great multitudes came together to hear, and to be healed by him of their infirmities. And he withdrew himself into the wilderness and prayed" (Luke 5:15-16).

Yes, men of power and fire have always been men of

prayer. Elijah prayed and, "*Then the fire of the Lord fell...*" (1 Kings 18:38). Elijah prayed and "*...the heaven was black with clouds and wind, and there was a great rain...*" (1 Kings 18:45). We know that John the Baptist was a man of prayer because he came in the spirit of Elijah. James, the brother of Jesus, was known as a praying man. Church history tells us that he was called "old camel knees" because of calluses that formed from long periods of kneeling in prayer. He wrote reverently of prayer, and his respect for the great prayer warrior is evident in James 5:16-18: "*...the effectual fervent prayer of a righteous man availeth much. Elijah was a man subject to like passions as we are, and he prayed earnestly that it might not rain: and it rained not on the earth by the space of three years and six months. And he prayed again, and the heaven gave rain, and the earth brought forth her fruit.*"

Men of fire are possessed of intense purpose and holy passion. The fiery zeal of such men, the life force flowing out from their burning hearts, stirs the slumbering church and awakens the saints to righteousness. One cannot be in the presence of such men, and not be impacted. To hear them preach is to be convicted to take action. Energy radiates from their spirits and the atmosphere around them is charged with holy passion and purpose. Why? They are men of power because they are men of prayer—men baptized in the Holy Ghost and fire.

Let us be done with this compromised, watered-down, Christianity of modern times. Let us be done with this pleasant, popular, polite religion without fire. Christianity is a religion of fire – of passion and purpose. Let us shake off this lethargic, lukewarm cloak of fireless experience and return to our first love. Let us flee from the cold complacency of half-hearted commitment, and run to the Lord with a love that demands all our heart, soul, strength and mind.

Christianity is a religion of fire – an all-consuming fire that spends itself in fervent devotion and joyful service to God. Real Christianity is a heart on fire, fueled with love for God and love for the lost. It is a heart filled with a holy desire to please God. It is a heart that goes forth to labor in the harvest fields of lost humanity crying, "*I delight to do thy will, O my God*" (Psalm 40:8). It is a heart moved with compassion for the lost (Matthew 9:36), pouring itself out on holy altars of sacrificial service. It is a heart so consumed with desire for God, so filled with the life of Another, it joyfully proclaims, "*It is no longer I that liveth, but Christ who liveth in me*" (Galatians

2:20).

New Testament Christianity knew nothing of the complacency and compromise of the church of our day. A gospel of fire, fueled by the oil of devotion, swept rapidly through the known world of the church born on the Day of Pentecost. It burned with the intensity of a heavenly mandate. It burned its way even into the court of Caesar, where it marked multitudes for heaven. Under the threat of death, converts with burning hearts renounced Caesar and owned Jesus as Lord.

Illumination, inspiration and dedication were the fruit of this fire. Trembling citizens of the Roman Empire were transformed into bold, blazing emissaries of heaven. Souls set on fire lost their affection for the things of earth and turned, with great longing and desire, their hearts toward heaven. Hearts so consumed cast themselves with complete abandon at the foot of the cross. They rose with renewed zeal and marched on toward Pentecost. At Pentecost, in the midst of the fire, they rose to embrace a high and holy purpose. They burned, and continued burning, consumed with the greatness of the cause that claimed them: the salvation of the lost. The

Holy Ghost came at Pentecost to fill the heart with power – power to witness. The fire that fell at Pentecost came to purify the empowered heart – purify it that the power poured out might flow through a holy vessel.

Nothing less than holy fire can purify the heart. Nothing less than holy fire can prevail over the corruption that is in the world through lust. Nothing less than holy fire can keep us "unspotted" from the contamination of ungodliness. Nothing less than holy fire can enable us to "be in the world but not of it."

Fireless Christianity is a feeble Christianity. We have endured enough of it. The darkness is pressing upon a dying world. The time is short. The days are evil. The harvest is ripe. The Spirit is ready. Are we willing? Will we crawl on, feeble and fireless, or will we march upward in faith and try Pentecost one more time?

Chapter Seventeen

The Return of the Real

Excitement accompanied the outpouring of the Holy Spirit at Pentecost. There was a great stir in the whole city. The excitement spread rapidly to surrounding regions as anointed, Holy Ghost preachers proclaimed the gospel in power. The early church had no need to rely on big-name preachers or entertainment to attract a crowd or cause a stir. The Spirit was moving, the word was being preached with signs following. The life of Jesus was being manifest. No other attraction was needed. Jesus was being lifted up and the Holy Spirit was drawing multitudes unto Him. The early church needed neither parties nor promotions. There were no gimmicks nor giveaways. Where the Spirit moved, the life of Christ was manifest and excitement resulted.

Think about the excitement that must have broken out when Peter fixed his eyes on the lame man at the gate of the Temple and in Jesus name told him to rise up and walk. Man's programs or promotions could never create excitement like that which broke out when the lame man went leaping and shouting and praising God. There was nothing boring about

New Testament Christianity. There is no need for man's programs or promotions when the shadow of a preacher moving over seriously sick and lame people results in their rising up with shouts of joy.

"And by the hands of the apostles were many signs and wonders wrought among the people; And believers were the more added to the Lord, multitudes both of men and women insomuch that they brought forth the sick into the streets, and laid them on beds and couches, that at the least the shadow of Peter passing by might overshadow some of them. There came also a multitude out of the cities round about unto Jerusalem, bringing sick folks, and them which were vexed with unclean spirits: and they were healed every one" (Acts 5:12, 14-16).

There was no need for theatrics in the midst of those excited multitudes. There were no attempts to create an artificial atmosphere with special lighting, special effects, and special music. No one was being "pushed down" in the Spirit. When people fell, they normally fell on their faces, not their backs. And they fell under God's power not man's pressure on their foreheads. There were no preachers running around with false fire calling it the anointing of the Holy Ghost. You could die for such deception in the holy air of Book of Acts

Christianity. The manipulations of fireless, powerless preachers of the modern church were not tolerated in the days of Peter and Paul. The early believers knew the difference between the brass and the gold. Powerless preachers soon had to sit down and shut up in such an atmosphere. Cheap substitutes are not welcomed where the authentic is experienced.

Can you picture the turmoil and excitement in Ephesus when seven religious leaders tried to cast out demons by imitating the methods of the Apostle Paul? Phonies were quickly exposed in an atmosphere charged with the power of the Holy Ghost. The Bible tells us that the demon possessed man beat up all seven, stripped them and chased them into the street saying, *"Jesus I know, and Paul I know; but who are you?"* (Acts 19:13-17).

Can we even begin to comprehend the level of excitement and expectation as multitudes witnessed the mighty power of God at work?

"And God wrought special miracles by the hands of Paul: so that from his body were brought unto the sick handkerchiefs or aprons,

and the diseases departed from them, and the evil spirits went out of them" (Acts 19:11-12). The whole city was in a stir. Revival was followed by riot. The foundations of hell were shaken. The powers of darkness were furious. Their former ally Saul, re-named Paul by the Holy Ghost, now became their worst nightmare. He who had once cooperated with demons in persecuting, torturing, and imprisoning Christians now tormented them with Holy Ghost power and authority: with preaching that healed the sick, drove out devils, raised the dead, and mended the broken-hearted. Time and time again the sinister forces of darkness hit him with all the fury of hell, but in every situation God delivered him. In every battle with demons, big and small, many or few, Paul emerged as more than a conqueror.

Try to imagine a lame man in the crowd, unable to get close to Paul. A concerned friend presses through the crowd and obtains a handkerchief Paul had used to wipe the sweat from his brow while preaching. The man gently places the handkerchief on his lame friend's chest and he immediately rises to his feet healed by virtue flowing out of a sweaty handkerchief. What joy, what excitement must have filled the cities where the great apostle preached. Today con-men, masquerading as preachers, sell prayer cloths to desperate people. There is no anointing on the man, much less on the cloth he sells, but with demonic subtlety these false prophets make merchandise of desperate people. What will it take to deliver us from the deceptions of such unrighteous men? When will the church, in holy revulsion, rise up and drive these ungodly imposters from among us? Why do we tolerate games and gimmicks when the genuine is offered to us?

With the return of the real, there will be a fresh baptism of power and fire. With the return of the real, the artificial will be identified and the imposters will be exposed. The fear of God will be resurrected in an atmosphere of holiness where liars will once again *"fall down and give up the ghost"* (Acts 5:5). This generation will not pass away without a testimony of power. The time is near when judgment must begin at the house of God. A fresh baptism of fire is imminent.

We must not allow the insidious influence of a counterfeit anointing to blind us to the real. The authentic pattern, inspired by the Holy Ghost and written down by men moved by Him, must be consulted. The standard is presented in the Book of Acts. Let we who discern the difference, not be discouraged. Let us not draw back in our quest for the genuine, in our pursuit of the true manifestation of the Holy Ghost. Let us read the New Testament accounts with expectation that God will do it again. Let us read, re-read and read again until faith rises in our hearts to cry, "Oh God please do it one more time!"

Ephesus was given over to darkness and wickedness. Witchcraft, Satanism, and all manner of curious arts were practiced. But all God needed to change that wicked city was a preacher – a genuine Holy Ghost-filled, fire-baptized preacher. Try to imagine the excitement in the city as Paul preached on their street corners, in their marketplaces, and before the temples of their false gods.

"And this was known to all the Jews and Greeks also dwelling at Ephesus, and fear fell on them all, and the name of the Lord Jesus was magnified. And many that believed came, and confessed and shewed their deeds. Many of them also which used curious arts brought their books together, and burned them before all men; and there was counted the price of them, and found it fifty thousand pieces of silver. So mightily grew the word of God and prevailed" (Acts 19:17-20).

God's word will also prevail in America. Revival will

come. It will, perhaps, be revival born out of judgment, but it will be revival nonetheless. It will come to those who refuse the counterfeit and wait for the real. It will come to those who reject the games and gimmicks and wait for the genuine. It will come to those who cry out for a fresh baptism of power accompanied by purifying fire from heaven's altar. It will come to those who in holy revulsion turn from man's programs and who, with complete abandon, pursue not the power of God but the God of power. It will come to those who say nothing else will do, nothing else will satisfy; therefore, I must try Pentecost one more time.

****

Made in the USA
San Bernardino, CA
24 June 2014